Clemmie Telford is a mother of three and the content creator behind the Mother of All Lists blog and the *Honestly* and *But Why?* podcasts. She spent the first thirteen years of her career as a Creative Director and Copywriter in top ad agencies and, most recently, at Facebook's Creative Shop. Her foray into social media began as a form of therapy whilst on maternity leave. Since then she has set about using her platforms to enable conversations about subjects that some might deem awkward or uncomfortable. Clemmie lives in Peckham, south-east London. She likes food, fitness and fashion and (ideally) not staying up too late.

BUT
WHY

How to Answer Tricky Questions from Kids
and Have an Honest Conversation with Yourself

CLEMMIE TELFORD

Foreword by Anna Mathur

First published in 2021
by Headline Home
an imprint of Headline Publishing Group

First published in paperback in 2022
by Headline Home
an imprint of Headline Publishing Group

1

Cataloguing in Publication Data is available from the British Library

ISBN 978 1 4722 7880 7
eISBN 978 1 4722 7879 1

Commissioning Editor: Lindsey Evans
Senior Editor: Kate Miles
Copy Editor: Lindsay Davies
Proofreaders: Amber Burlinson and Jill Cole
Indexer: Caroline Wilding

Designed and typeset by EM&EN
Printed and bound in Great Britain by Clays Ltd, Elcograf S.p.A.

MIX
Paper from
responsible sources
FSC® C104740

Headline's policy is to use papers that are natural, renewable and recyclable
products and made from wood grown in well-managed forests and other
controlled sources. The logging and manufacturing processes are expected
to conform to the environmental regulations of the country of origin.

HEADLINE PUBLISHING GROUP
An Hachette UK Company
Carmelite House
50 Victoria Embankment
London EC4Y 0DZ

www.headline.co.uk
www.hachette.co.uk

For Bertie, Woody & Greta.
My three favourite curious minds.
Thank you for being the answer to
questions I didn't know I had.

CONTENTS

3: QUESTIONS ABOUT RELATIONSHIPS

4: QUESTIONS ABOUT COMPLEX FEELINGS

5: QUESTIONS ABOUT WORK AND MONEY

6: MISCELLANEOUS QUESTIONS

7: THE BIG QUESTIONS

FOREWORD

As a psychotherapist, I welcome questions from my clients, but when they come from my kids, I am filled with fear of 'getting it wrong'. *But Why?* places sturdy hands upon my shoulders. It has cultivated a bravery within myself to face the questions that I often feel a rising temptation to sidestep.

A few months ago, absent-mindedly scrolling on my phone in the passenger seat of the car, my ears suddenly tuned in to something my husband said to our son in the back. I wasn't sure of the context as I hadn't been listening, but I heard: 'You do know that Mummy and Daddy made you?'

My head whipped round to face him, wide-eyed and startled. I held my breath, waiting for the questions to come. 'But why? But how?'

I diverted attention by whipping out a scratched CD from under the seat, and the questions didn't arrive. I breathed a sigh of relief.

It made me think, though; we need to be prepared for the questions to come. And even if I don't have a solid answer up my cheese-sandwich-crumbed sleeve, I need to expect them and to be open to them instead of shrugging them off or distracting their course to somewhere more comfortable.

I aim to not be fearful of the questions, at least. I am my kids' navigator during these years. They turn to me for safety, to have their needs met, and most importantly to help them make sense of the world around them.

And sometimes, guiding them to make sense of the world around them will include acknowledging the uncertainty, the unknowns, the lack of right or wrongs, the grey areas. Plus the fact that they are free to form an opinion that may differ from mine.

Whatever they look to me for, I want to welcome their enquiry, rather than scrabble to flee from it. As they see us head to vote with ballot cards in our hands, as they are introduced to Leo's two mums. As they meet a child in the playground who doesn't move in the same way as they do.

As a psychotherapist, I have spent thousands of hours welcoming the questions of clients as they explore and form their own world view. For how we see the world is both changed by what we already know, and changed by our new insights too. I have seen lives transformed by the questions my clients have asked me, as they sat upon my blue sofa, but also the questions they have asked themselves.

So why, then, do I find it so challenging to hold the space as my kids seek my support to guide them, to dig through what we know and what we don't? To sit with uncertainty, to feel angered at new realisations about the planet, to feel hurt at rejection, and to push and question the boundaries drawn around them by me, by society.

I think it's because I have a deep fear of 'getting it wrong', which I am consistently trying to overcome. 'Presence over perfection' is my new mantra, and what greater way to challenge myself in this, in my motherhood, than to desire to be present with their questioning, no matter how big or small, and regardless of how much I know, or don't.

I am not all-knowing; I am not perfect. I am a few years down the road in age from them, with a little more experience under my belt, of course, but they don't need me to regurgitate cold, hard facts like a human Wikipedia with a ponytail; they do not need me to give a crisp and confident answer. They do not need perfect; they need present. They need me to sit with them and grapple with the hard questions, to muse on them and put my hands up when quite frankly, I don't know. But they also need me to have asked myself some of these questions so that I can share what I do know, as well as what I don't.

I have always admired Clemmie's courage to 'go there'. To ask herself the questions, to facilitate and welcome conversation around the sticky topics and, most powerfully, not to shy away from challenge or taboo. The very nature of taboo and sidestepping very valid questioning (especially from a child as they seek to navigate and make sense of the world) tells us that we should feel shame about the not-knowing. Taboo is silencing; it halts enquiry and creates 'no-go zones'. We learn to toe the line, stick to the common paths and can end up denying our own thoughts and opinions.

Having spent years unpicking my own learned need to fall in line, to nod along, to swerve, I want more for my kids than this. I want them to find value in the questioning, in the way the world opens up when you challenge prejudice and structures. For the way the brain's synapses fizz and reform when we become pliable to having our opinions grown by welcoming the differing experiences and stories of others. Life becomes richer when we welcome enquiry and difference, and are willing to challenge and be challenged.

But Why? invites it all. It's an aid for parents to help them welcome explorations around the big questions, the small questions and all the feelings that come with them. It's a comforting and supportive 'let's do this', a hand on your shoulder as you search wildly for a scratched CD to distract. It's a toolbox, a buffet of food for thought so you can have those conversations over dinner tables with friends should you want them, before you are blindsided on a Tuesday morning as you pack crisps into schoolbags.

But most of all, *But Why?* is the breaking down of the taboo. The tearing away of the 'keep out' tape cordoning certain conversations. Encouraging enquiry and openness, a loving learning rather than a shutting-down. A better imperfect and subjective as opposed to the churning-out of an A* answer. Because really, it's all about presence over perfection, connection over correction.

Thank you, Clemmie. This book is going to support me in giving to my children what I have so confidently been giving my clients. Adventure lies outside of our comfort zones, so for them, and for me, I must continue to step out of mine.

Anna Mathur

✳ INTRODUCTION ✳

Cut a long story short, I don't have the answers. None of them.

At which point you're probably wondering why you bothered picking up the book. Which is in itself a good question. Maybe you were looking for spiritual or moral guidance in the form of 'answering big questions'.

Sorry to disappoint. I will level with you. Let's get it all out on the table, then we all know where we are at and I don't have to pretend, which would be hard to maintain for the following 70,000 words.

First of all, why did I set out on this 'journey' (a horribly over-used word, but there doesn't seem to be a better one)? Before I had kids, I was naïve. I thought I knew how life-changing parenting was going to be. I didn't. I thought I had lived a fair bit before having kids. I hadn't. I was thirty when I had Bertie and we had done a lot of the normal stuff – but boy, was I unlived and unprepared!

I could easily imagine, pre-kids, that Ben, my husband, would be good at the fun elements of parenting: the den-building, superhero, sporty bits. Whereas I *fully* backed myself to be excellent at the parts that involved 'answering big questions'. Perhaps because I considered myself to be worldly and informed and (before my brain got ruined by babies) I loved throwing around ideas and philosophising about the whys and wherefores of existence. I'd even done a very intellectual (cough cough) degree in Drama, Culture and Media Studies to prove it. So naturally I couldn't wait to help nurture the precious minds of those (at that point imaginary) kids I would create.

I was wrong.

As is the case with everything in parenting (and, frankly, in life), the reality is nothing like you imagine.

It's Tuesday night. But it feels like at least Thursday. I have hummus on my top. I have a million emails to answer and, while I have bathed three kids, I still have to negotiate bedtime with two of them. My period's due. And I'm hungry.

And then a sweet, innocent and curious voice pipes up from the sofa: 'But why do people die and are they just sleeping?

Really? I think. *Are we doing this now?*

Not only do I want to hop-skip away from ONE OF LIFE'S TRICKY QUESTIONS towards the tantalisingly close scenario of my children being in bed and me sitting down to eat my favourite quiche, I also don't have a clue what to say.

Could this be the moment when my well-meaning but ultimately slapdash answer screws over my (occasionally) darling children and results in them ending up in therapy for years on end? And if so, how on earth do I avoid this outcome?

As well as being less-than-adept at answering the 'but why?' questions from my kids, the other thing I got wrong is the whole premise of this book.

The plan behind it was a simple one: pick the biggest, most common, most thorny issues. Set aside several months of research and really get to the bottom of them and come back with some solid answers.

2

This did not happen.

The more I learned, the further I dug, the less knowledgeable I became. If it were possible to be minus knowledgeable, that is where I was at. In addition, this research period perfectly coincided with us being hit by a global pandemic. I began writing in early April 2020 – what a great project to undertake during lockdown, right?

Wrong! (Are you sensing a theme here?)

There are many things to learn from Covid-19, but one of them is that spending months at home, surrounded by kids, no longer able to hug friends and family and with no certain plan of what is in store is a sure way to find yourself questioning everything you thought you knew.

Cue existential crisis.

And that's not even an exaggeration – there was a particularly low moment involving a whiteboard, a multi-pack of pens and me trying to 'crack' the concept of 'why we don't feel happy all the time' on too many coffees and not enough sleep. Yes, I was literally crying over the concept of joy!

I digress.

The more I learned, the less I knew. And the more glaringly obvious it was that googling the answers could not and should not cut it.

Instead I looked to the Stoics, who seem to know a thing or two about life. They helped me back on track by reminding me that it is okay not to know. Maybe that means I am on the right track to enlightenment. 'It is impossible to begin to learn that which one thinks one already knows,' said Epictetus. Which is a good thing to remember in order to fight that knee-jerk reaction. However, just because you don't know, doesn't mean you can opt out. This is a 'brush it under the carpet' approach that might have been common in previous generations – but we can do better.

I also sought solace in other people's anxiety, by asking how other parents felt about answering their kids' tricky questions. I quickly realised that it's not just me feeling daunted. Is that a good or bad thing? Not sure, but 87 per cent of those I surveyed in my research (see below) worried that they weren't getting the answers right.

Many people were delighted by their children's curiosity but concerned by their own lack of knowledge, a difficulty finding the right language and both a fear of potentially getting it wrong and also being judged by others for getting it wrong.

Many were debilitated by the pressure that what they might say could be offensive to someone else, fear of their own unconscious bias, and that projecting their beliefs onto their children could prevent them from creating their own. Yup. Yup. Yup.

Also, many said kids have a knack of catching you by surprise, and asking you difficult questions at the wrong moment.

And then there is the tightrope that needs to be trodden between wanting to avoid hiding things from them but not wanting to overwhelm them either; the battle between trying to solve their issues for them and wanting them to have the tools to find solutions themselves. So we are all worried about the 'but why?'s. Now what are we going to do about it?

Panic!

Then be rational (and momentarily serious). Much of this book is informed by the hours and hours of conversations I've been lucky enough to have on my podcasts *Honestly* and *But Why?*, but also the 300-plus contributors who have written for my blog Mother of All Lists, bravely sharing a first-hand account of an experience.

Not to mention the huge network of people willing to open up on Instagram, often in ways that leave me humbled and amazed. In fact, periodically you'll see me refer to my own 'research' – to be clear, that is me using Instagram Stories to 'ask the audience'. Votes and submissions come direct to me, rather than being public, which I believe makes people very truthful in their responses (by truthful, I mean 'absolutely unfiltered'). I asked about different subjects at different times, therefore the pool of responses varied but broadly ranged from 2,000 to 5,000 in number.

Between all these channels I've been in a unique position of having had access to a vast array of insights to draw on when looking for the answers to any questions. Plus I have supplemented all this with a mountain of supporting study and my own experience as a mother of three.

That's my bit, but I also have an idea of how I hope *you* will approach this. Remember in maths we were always told to show our workings? That's how I'd like you to see this book.

Or think of it like cooking. I rarely follow a single recipe when cooking. Instead I read through a few different ideas by various cooks and take the bits of them I like, bearing in mind a) what I have in the fridge, and b) what I fancy, and one way or another I end up with a version that works. And then next time I might try something a bit different.

In here you'll find a smorgasbord of pointers and perspectives to add to your experiences. Nothing is prescriptive or definitive; they're just there for you to pick from when and if you fancy.

Between the answers to all those 'but why?' questions, you'll find what I am unscientifically calling 'joining bits'. They are the tools and techniques that I have found help me to answer tricky questions. You might consider them 'guiding principles for self-discovery' – but that sounds horrendous, so let's stick with 'joining bits'.

When setting about answering tricky questions it's vital to check two things: 1) your sources, and 2) your assumptions. Assumptions can be dangerous. Cognitive Behavioural Therapy (CBT) was fundamental in helping me learn to help myself by enabling me to recognise my own thought patterns and giving me the tools to rationalise them. Because thoughts are not facts.

I hope there will be a similar process at play for you here. No knee-jerk answers. Instead this is an invitation to stop and think. In her book, *Purpose,*[1] Jessica Huie calls out the fact that we all start out as blank canvases but soon our parents unconsciously begin to mould us. Their fears, opinions and version of truth become ours. This is why it sometimes feels like perspectives aren't moving at all. That out-of-date comment from your mate about a gay person is shocking, but often it's not their voice you're really hearing; it's a lingering generational hangover.

Huie uses the analogy of a car: by the time we reach adulthood, the boot is so full of baggage that our vehicles can hardly power up. We can all well imagine that Tetris-style image in which no family trip happens without squeezing stuff into every available space in the back of the car.

Our job as adults is to sort through all that stuff and ask ourselves if we really need or want to keep carrying it with us. It's easier said than done to unburden ourselves and challenge our own perspectives in the name of growth. Which is why many choose to ignore it and instead slam the boot shut and keep going.

But, as Philippa Perry taught us in *The Book You Wish Your Parents Had Read*[2] – whether we like it or not, we are going to shape our kids. I would suggest that it's better we do that when we aren't burdened with a load of bags we might not even need.

The other concept I have been drawn to while writing this book is the idea that you should aim to give your child what is known as 'emotional privilege', and how it is the nectar of love. It comes in a few guises, including shielding our children from our own anxieties and being able to enter into their imaginative world. It also extends to being honest with them.

I believe there are huge benefits to our children knowing that we don't always have the answers. It's not 'I don't know and that's a worry' because we want them to feel stable and secure. We want them to hear, 'I don't know and I am going to find out.' Rather than aiming to 'know it all', we must be forever learning.

My granny was already nearly blind when she got her first computer. She wasn't embarrassed about the fact that her emails were riddled with mistakes when her original meaning was mangled by the voice-recognition technology. No way, José. She was wise enough to know the odd mistake was a small price to pay for the benefit of the sense of connection that email brought her.

But what my granny and her generation didn't do was google the answers, or resort to asking someone they followed on the internet (oh the irony).

So we need to be willing to get it wrong or admit when we've reached the limit of our knowledge, but at the same time we do need to try to find *some* kind of sensible response when our child lobs us yet another curveball. But how do we do that, when faced with an impossible question at an impossible moment?

My main piece of advice when answering any question is to *buy yourself time*. I will tell you why. First, in many instances the questions are nothing more than a ruse aimed at trying to deflect or delay you from the task in hand. Common scenarios include (but are not limited to) bedtime, putting on shoes and eating a healthy meal you lovingly prepared.

Second, you rarely give your best answers when reactive rather than contemplative. Or when you are tired/stressed/hungry/unprepared. But buying time doesn't mean you shouldn't come back to the question later.

Oh, and the questions themselves? The ones you will find in this book have come from all over: many from my kids, many from conversations I've had with parents and guardians both online and in real life. Not to mention my WhatsApp group with my best uni mates: once upon a time we used to tear up the streets of Bristol partying – now we limp through the struggles of being parents while trying not to kill our partners and hoping to keep a sense of ourselves.

One person messaged to say their young kid had pulled her aside to enquire, 'What is a gang bang?' Yup, I may have sniggered A LOT reading that. And in this instance I am going to leave you to answer that one yourselves. Soz.

The questions I have included in the chapters that follow are a starting point to covering the big stuff. Not definitively or conclusively. I split them into broad subsections – but as you will see they all end up relating to one another because really you can't talk about death without love, or money without gender. I don't quite go as far as answering, 'What is the meaning of life?' but 70,000 words in, it felt as if I had.

And even then, maybe the meaning of life is attempting to prepare the next generation for experiences outside of our own. Or at least learning when a question comes from a curious mind and when it's just a delay tactic to avoid bedtime.

Speaking of bedtime, remember the days when you were young and could stay up until the sun rose, talking to someone and putting the world to rights? I used to love hearing all their stuff, trying to absorb it and using it as a lens to understand my stuff.

These days I am fairly passionate about being in bed by 10.30 p.m. But although the sunrise session with a pack of Marlboro Lights is behind me, I still thrive on collecting anecdotes as well as all the bigger insights. So, while I was writing this book, I asked all sorts of people to complete the sentence: 'When I was young, I wish I had known that . . .'

You'll find their answers dotted between sections, like little bonuses: a pound down the back of a sofa, or an ancient but still edible kid's snack lurking at the bottom of your bag when you have forgotten to have breakfast and find yourself hangry. Okay, I lied, I have never missed breakfast. But I do like finding forgotten snacks. And I do like these snacky insights from excellent people.

Okay. Another preamble. Let's do this . . .

When I was a kid, I wish I had known that . . . there are other ways to learn, that everyone takes in and retains information differently, emotional intelligence is just as valid and needed to be successful as IQ. Find the way you like to learn and build your education around this. I love the quote attributed to Einstein: 'Everyone is a genius. But if you judge a fish by its ability to climb a tree, it will live its whole life believing that it is stupid.'

Nina Malone @dopeblackmums

1

QUESTIONS ABOUT THE BIG WIDE WORLD

BUT WHY DO WE HAVE
A PRIME MINISTER AND
WHAT DO THEY DO?

This seems like a punchy place to start, but that's generally how I roll. The more scared I am of something, the more likely I am to jump in feet first and try to get it over with. Which is also why I did not take kindly to going really overdue with ALL of my kids – Bertie was 41 weeks + 6 days and Greta and Woody were 41 + 1. The only thing I can compare it to is standing at the start line of a marathon knowing that you are going to run it, but being unable to start (for transparency, I've never actually run a marathon. Ha! But you get the analogy). I am all about getting on with it and figuring it out on the go. Which actually in the case of these questions is absolutely the worst thing you can do, so maybe scrap that.

When I think of the big wide world, I think of Oliver Jeffers' brilliant kids' book, *Here We Are*.[3] 'Well, hello. Welcome to this planet. We call it Earth. It is the big globe, floating in space, on which we live . . . There is much to see and do here on Earth, so let's get started . . .'

BUT WHY DO WE HAVE
A PRIME MINISTER AND
WHAT DO THEY DO?

Somewhere along the line I was told that there were certain topics that should never be discussed: religion, money and politics. Whoever came up with that is plain wrong. The best gift we can give ourselves is the guts to talk about the hard stuff. The more we avoid the difficult issues, the more damage we do, as it means we make things taboo. To my mind, even the notion of taboo is ludicrous – sharing ideas and opinions is how we learn.

Politics impacts everything, so why wouldn't we talk about it? Crucially, when I begin open conversations about politics it's not with the objective of converting anyone to my way of thinking but more as a lens to better understand their view of the world. I intend to make politics part of our family's normal conversation. I want my kids to be curious and to invest time and energy into exploring their own political beliefs.

So where to begin?

Well, as usual, I suggest we start by keeping it simple and to my mind the resource doing that best is Simple Politics, whose easy-to-digest Instagram feed has been a guiding light for me, just to understand the foundations of politics. So I reached out to founder Tatton Spiller, who gave the following advice:

How to explain basic politics to your kids:

- At an election, each political party (such as the Conservatives, Labour, Lib Dems, etc) has a leader. They're the ones who wander round the country telling everyone to vote for them.

- The leader of the party who gets the most votes and wins that election becomes the Prime Minister (PM) and moves into Number 10 Downing Street.

- They also inherit Larry, the cat who lives at Number 10.

- Once there, they run the country.

- The first thing they do is give jobs to the people that they would like to run each individual bit, such as the NHS, or education or the police.

- The PM then sets out what they want to happen and what they want the country to look like.

- It's their team who do most of the work looking after their departments.

- They think about all sorts of questions, like how are we going to make sure everyone has enough money, or should the NHS focus on disease or cancer or mental health, or what makes a good school. That kind of thing.

- At the end of the day, it all comes back to the Prime Minister. They have to explain why they took the right decision at the right time.

- They also have a job travelling round the world, showing what a great country we are, and what a great and reliable leader they are.

- The idea is to persuade people to spend lots of money in our country, making more jobs and more money to spend.

- A Prime Minister gives a face to the people who run the country. They are one person who is responsible for absolutely everything. A school runs out of money? What are they going to do about it? Too many people are losing their jobs? Come on, Prime Minister, what's the plan?

• Not only are they in charge, but they can be questioned by others. Each week they have Prime Minister's Questions, when MPs can ask questions about anything they want.

• That makes them accountable – they have to show their workings-out. Marks can be given there, even if the plan doesn't work out.

• It also helps that they need to be re-elected every few years. If they don't do a good job, the country can give them the boot and get someone else in.

• Away from the UK, it really helps to have one face that everyone knows is our leader.

• They can potter off to, say, Colombia and shake hands and agree on sharing stuff. People love it when our PM visits them. Normally.

• Why are they so important? Because somebody needs to be accountable and make the decisions!

Even as a thirty-eight-year-old I am not ashamed to admit that there's something really useful in having things spelled out like that. My research told me that 91 per cent of people wanted to better understand politics, by which they meant comprehending the actual processes of government as opposed to party politics. I admit that it's not easy to find truly unbiased information on this, but Simple Politics is a brilliant starting point.

When I caught up with Tatton for my *But Why?* podcast he explained that though many cited the need for better political education in school, he felt that was potentially misguided.

The comparison he gave is that teaching kids politics in school is like expecting sex education involving a condom on a carrot to equip a generation who have access to porn at the tap of a finger. It's a great point.

But what's the alternative? Well, one outcome of the Covid pandemic is that kids up and down the country will have seen or even been part of gathering round the TV to watch Boris *et al* give their briefings. Experiencing the fact that government has the power to 'lock down' the country will have shown them how important politics is.

My own childhood realisation of that was less extreme but I did grow up in a house where politics was discussed quite freely, and I recall feeling excited on the first election day I can remember. It was when John Major was voted in, so April 1992 – I would have been ten. I wasn't excited because of the outcome or the politics itself but because I was taught that elections are significant moments. Since then I have voted with purpose in every election.

For Tatton, the future of politics rests in teaching tolerance and in showing kids how to think critically and have meaningful conversations. I couldn't agree more, and I hope to be able to help with some of that in the following chapters. But also I feel strongly that my kids should feel informed, proud and inspired to vote.

Our right to vote is one of the greatest privileges and one that I want my kids to a) appreciate, and b) understand. It's up to us to communicate the importance of politics to the next generation.

We need to be providing the tools for tolerance and good, open conversation. And, to go back to the notion of taboo, there is some logic to say that if a chat feels difficult it is probably the one most worth having.

BUT WHY ARE HUMANS
RUINING THE PLANET?

A 2019 report by the UN concluded: 'Human actions threaten more species with global extinction now than ever before.' That's a weighty thing to sit with.

We need to be realistic about the damage that can be caused by the machines we have built. The real answer to the question about humans ruining the planet lies in action and what we are going to do about it.

Teenage activist Greta Thunberg called for us to panic about the climate crisis. Our kids and their kids are going to be paying the price. She similarly told us that no one is too small to make a difference.

There is hope – but it does not come from the governments or corporations, it comes from the people.

'The people who have been unaware are now starting to wake up, and once we become aware we change,' said Greta. 'We can change and people are ready for change. And that is the hope, because we have democracy.'

Don't make it all sound doom and gloom when you talk about this subject with your children. Relate it back to them. Tell them about Greta. Help them to make small changes that make a difference.

I got in touch with Frida Berry Eklund, the founder of the climate-parent network Our Kids' Climate, and the author of the upcoming book *Talk to Children about Climate Change: A Handbook for Parents*. Frida is a wealth of information and shared a bunch of age-appropriate insights on how we should talk about the 'planetary crisis' (to borrow a phrase from her) to children:

- **Nursery-age children** are too young to understand that a forest fire in Australia isn't happening in the same place as where they are, for instance. Global issues and extreme weather can be big and very scary. Instead, my best advice for nursery-age children is to keep stimulating their connection to – and understanding of – nature and our eco systems. And of course, making planetary care part of our everyday lives.

- **For school-age children** (starting from about seven), we can use simple explanations about global problems. We can talk about how the blanket around the planet is getting thicker, making the planet hotter, what causes it, and what some of the solutions are. Today, the planet has a fever but we can all help cool it down. It's good to talk about national or even local impacts and solutions, making the issue closer to home. And talk about what we can do ourselves to act. This is a great age to get kids to imagine/draw/create the world they want to see when they grow up.

- **For teens**, we need to be there to talk when *they* want to. A good way is to ask what they know about the climate crisis, or what Greta Thunberg is all about. Asking questions is a good way to find out how they are feeling about the issue. Are they feeling disempowered and hopeless about the future? Let's support them to find ways to act, together with others.

On a broader level, she advised that we should be honest without giving false assurance. After all, she says, 'We don't know that [it will be okay]; it will depend on our actions in the next few years.' We should reassure our children that the responsibility to solve this is on us adults (gulp), whilst also making kids aware that we are all able to help with the solutions – no one is too young to get involved.

Personally, I tend to shy away from the 'wrapping kids up in cotton wool' approach to parenting. I want to prepare them for the big wide world rather than shield them from it. Also, I have always wondered, if you opt to protect them from reality, when is it okay to rip the metaphorical band-aid off? 'Happy eighteenth birthday and welcome to adulthood! Here's the hard truth we kept from you.' Ha!

Tackling the weighty topics is likely to evoke strong emotions. That's okay, assures Frida. 'Being sad, upset or frustrated is a healthy reaction to the state of the world.' Here are things that can help and some pitfalls to avoid:

1. Focus on the importance of channelling the uncomfortable feelings into action. This could be supporting a green organisation, advocating for change in your local community or starting a climate group at school.

2. Don't push the issue too hard if your child doesn't want to talk about it. This can have the unintended effect of actually turning them off the topic. Instead, keep acting for the climate and show your child that you are part of the solution. Walk the talk!

3. Be wary of the fact that showing climate-related news, for instance of extreme weather events, can be too frightening. Instead look specifically for positive stories about people doing good things for the planet.

4. Just talk, with no corresponding action, is no use. We need to show our children that this is an issue we care deeply about and that we are ready to do our bit.

5. Avoid giving assurances that everything will be okay. The truth is we don't know exactly how bad it's going to be if we continue with business as usual.

How you and your family can change your consumption habits for the better:

Someone else who helped me become more clued up on this subject was Sophie of @trashplastic, who is also a member of Extinction Rebellion.

Sophie and I met via DMs where, over a polite but heated exchange, she made me realise that my 'enough' in relation to climate change was actually far from it. It wasn't comfortable to accept, but it was a turning point for me, and I vowed to do better.

Before we got into the ins and outs of the practical changes you can make with your family, Sophie caveated that she feared being vocal about climate change would make for unpopular reading. An admission like that is music to my ears: the awkward stuff is nearly always the most valuable. So here goes.

For Sophie, the best place to start is to take inspiration from Maya Angelou, whose ethos is to 'do the best you can, until you know better', and crucially 'when you know better, do better'.

Like most, Sophie was doing her bit, but a few years ago something shifted. A combination of watching *Blue Planet* (more on the significance of Attenborough later) and learning that by 2050 there will be more plastic in the ocean than fish were the spurs to action.

'When you know better, do better.' From there she set a goal of using 80 per cent less plastic. How? The first step was to get a sense of how bad her family's plastic problem was. So they saved every bit of plastic they used for a week.

Sophie washed it, stashed it, then at the end of the week, tipped it out and surveyed the reality of their consumption. The amount made her cry! It made me wonder if I have the guts to do the same. Would you?

What next? Here's some great advice: 'When you know where most of your plastic comes from, tackling those things first will make the most difference. There's no point stressing about a deodorant that gets bought every few months, if there are plastic-wrapped bananas in the weekly shop.' Relatively straightforward swaps might include ordering milk from a milkman or buying cat food in tins rather than pouches.

From thereon, Sophie talks of being rigorous with questioning how she shopped – trying to puncture her behaviour, which by her own admission had become a matter of operating on autopilot rather than conscious choice. 'While we're creatures of habit,' she says, 'we're creatures that can change our habits too.'

The uncomfortable truth is that it's the relentless pursuit of 'more' that 'is driving this bus', says Sophie. 'Every bit of data modelling shows that to be impossible. If the global economy continues to shoot for 3 per cent growth, it's also shooting for 3 degrees – and fast. And this is the stuff of nightmares.'

Einstein said, 'We cannot solve our problems with the same thinking we used when we created them.'

After looking at plastic consumption, look to your carbon footprint, suggests Sophie. It's easy to think of this in terms of energy suppliers and travel choices, but our carbon footprint is hiding in EVERYTHING we buy, eat and do.

We all have a carbon budget, based on the emissions targets outlined in the Paris Climate Accord. There is a good foot-print calculator on the WWF website. This could be a good activity to do with your child: answer the questions together and see how you are doing. You'll likely be surprised by the breadth of the things involved. Have you bought a new piece of furniture in the last year? How much do you spend on food from cafés and restaurants? How much do you spend on clothes?

Much like collecting the plastic, this was a turning point for Sophie: she realised she could do things differently, simply by buying less. She puts it like this:

'Less #yolo, less #fomo, less #ootd, less #livingmybestlife, less #whatiworetoday. Less craving, less comparing, less consuming, less buying. Less fast fashion, less single-use anything. Less meat, less dairy, less plastic, less waste. Less flying, less driving, less stuff. Because the bonkers thing is, there is masses of scientific evidence that shows that embracing "less" actually makes us HAPPIER.

'By appreciating what we already have, living with less clutter, slowing down, being more mindful, choosing carefully, finding joy in small pleasures and real human interactions, we are MORE, not less, fulfilled. Less "stuffocation" = more happiness.' She then adds, 'I feel driven to do right by the planet, but also a huge sense of relief in stepping back from the relentless pursuit of keeping up with the Kardashian-Joneses . . . You would have to have been living under a rock to have not seen the powerful speeches by Greta Thunberg. She has inspired millions of other children to rise up and fight for their futures. And her language is crystal clear. "I want you to act as if the house is on fire. Because it is."'

All this is so big to compute, isn't it?

The simple answer to the question 'But why are humans ruining the planet?' is that we have been too focused on what we want, rather than thinking about what the planet needs.

However, it isn't as clear cut as that. I wanted to point to the fact that of the 3,000 people I surveyed on Instagram, 9 per cent said that environmentalism wasn't a priority for them. One person simply put it as 'I can't be everything for everyone'. The majority cited money as the issue. Cost and time are the biggest barriers: *'Being environmentally friendly is often a privilege . . . I'd love to buy more sustainably but sometimes my budget stops me . . . Small personal changes are pointless when 70 per cent of emissions come from 100 companies . . . The best choice is often the most expensive . . . Companies don't take it seriously, why should we as individuals? . . . I am barely keeping my head above water; I do what I can but struggle to do more.'*

I would suggest there is a middle value between the Maya Angelou quote and where you are at personally. Do the best you can until you know better and so do the best with where you are at.

For me, I don't want to be handing the world over to the next generation in a far worse state than when we found it. Often I lose sight of the problem – sometimes that's because there is SO much else to deal with (hello, Covid-19); other times it's because it can seem abstract. A great leveller is the man, the myth, the legend: Sir David Attenborough, and his series *Extinction: The Facts*.

The fact that now, after his frankly epic career, Sir David, who has seen (and shared) more of the natural world than almost anyone, is driven to tell us of the million species at risk of extinction, and how this crisis of biodiversity has consequences for us all, threatening food and water security, undermining our ability to control our climate and even putting us at greater risk of pandemic disease, is both terrifying and moving. When we hear that famous voice say, 'What happens next is up to every one of us', it really sticks.

BUT WHY DO PEOPLE HAVE DIFFERENT HAIR/EYES/SKIN?

Later (page 54) we discuss how kids are keen to appear to 'be like everyone else', but what about differences? Why do they exist and what are the wider implications of that?

Did you know no two snowflakes are the same? It's the same thing with people. Even those identical twins that look really alike, chances are if you look closely there will be tiny differences between them.

Hair texture is down to the shape of follicles. Straight hair comes out of round follicles, curly hair from oval follicles. The flatter the oval is, the curlier the hair. Hair can change texture with age, or from stress or medicine.

Hair colour is set from conception. Wikipedia flags that the genetic basis of hair colour is complex and not fully understood, which makes it unlikely that me and my very un-scientific mind will be able to convey much beyond the basics to you (and my kids). The bottom line is, hair colour is down to genes and the relative amounts of two types of melanin: eumelanin and pheomelanin.

With eye colour I stumbled on a bunch of fascinating facts. Again, answering any kid's question with science can be a great place to start. It's believed that up to 10,000 years ago, all humans had brown eyes only. Then a mutation turned off the pigmentation on the front of the iris for some people.

Babies born with brown eyes stay brown-eyed. Blue-eyed babies can change: sunlight stimulates melanin production and so the colour changes in the first year and can in some cases even continue changing into adulthood (fancy that!).

Only about 2 per cent of the world's population has green eyes (including me). The reason is in our genes, which determine how much of the pigment melanin they produce. The more we produce, the darker the eye colour. Melanin will also influence your skin colour and that varies from person to person.

You might want to leave it at that. However, this could also be an opportunity for a wider conversation about race, and with that comes the trickier subject of racism.

Now, it's common to feel an urge to shy away from talking about racism. When opening up the research about this, some people felt that it wasn't necessary to talk to kids about this subject and that it might cause problems where there weren't any.

To counter that, perhaps consider a few other things:

1. Your kids will likely be exposed to news and conversations about racism whether you like it or not. Dunno about you, but I'd always rather they learned as much as possible from me, rather than a random Tom, Donna or Harry.

2. Those who are at the receiving end of racism don't have the luxury of opting out of the conversation.

3. Forty per cent of 3,000 people who responded to my research admitted that they didn't feel confident talking about the subject. Is that what is preventing the chat?

Research by Caryn Park, a professor at Antioch University in Seattle, on children's understanding of race and ethnicity showed that children as young as three years old are aware of skin colour. Skin colour first came up in our home when my second son, Woody, was a year or so old. Woody has inherited my olive complexion while Bertie has Ben's far fairer skin. Bertie asked why he and his bro looked so different from one another. This conversation actually still comes up every now and again, especially since Greta is also olive-y too. It's moments like this that can be a good opportunity to throw open a discussion on the subject.

Also, while it's never too early to talk about race, it's also not too late. More on that shortly in relation to the imaginary 'Great Uncle John'.

Race, racism, discrimination and inequality:

Even that combination of words on a page is big. It's big, it's nuanced, it's emotional and it is important. All the more reason to try to get it right. But also all the more reason to put my hands up to say I probably won't. But I do know that I have approached it in good faith. Better to try and risk needing correcting than to bury your head in the sand by remaining silent.

Though every family's conversation around race will take a different shape, there are guiding principles that are likely to be the same.

A great starting point is Martin Luther King's famous quote: 'I have a dream that my four little children will one day live in a nation where they will not be judged by the colour of their skin, but by the content of their character.'

No-brainer, right?

Racism is abhorrent.

Nobody, anybody, should be perpetuating behaviour that looks or feels like white supremacy. It must be wiped out.

But how do we bridge the gap between where we are now and where we want to be, so that we keep moving towards greater equality? For me the basics look like this:

What should every kid know about race?

- There is only one human race but there are different cultures and identities within it.

- Some people have a different experience of life because of their skin and that is wrong – we all look the same underneath.

- The universal thing every kid should know is that the simplest rule is to be kind, even if others look different from them.

- Race has been used throughout history to make people seem different. The world still isn't fair; we must help to make it fair.

- We are different and alike at the same time and that can play a part in challenging racism.

- Some people are jerks, so we need to stand up for those who can't stand up for themselves.

- We have come some way towards equality but still have a long way to go. Ask questions, keep learning.

And then consider helping your kid understand some specific terms they might hear.

Race is the idea that the human species (that's us!) can be divided into distinct groups on the basis of inherited physical traits that they are perceived to share.

Racism means that not everyone is treated the same. It shouldn't exist but it does and there is still work to be done and changes to be made to make sure everyone is judged by their character, not their skin colour.

Discrimination is when someone is treated unfairly or differently. That can be for a number of reasons, but in the context of this question we are talking about potential discrimination because of skin colour.

Another term they may encounter is **white privilege**. That refers to the notion that if you are white and you're raising kids in a place where the large majority of the population is white, you benefit from certain advantages that those who aren't white don't have. Yes, there are other things that may hold you back but in this case race isn't one of them. You have not had to live in a society within the constraints of racism. I like the way author Sophie Williams of @officialmillennialblack talks about it: 'Having privilege doesn't mean that everything in your life has been easy, it just means that there are some areas where you haven't had to struggle whilst others have.'

Focus on the idea of fairness:

Racism is the opposite of fairness.

Aged five and seven, my boys have already shown an understanding of disparity via the hugely important medium of 'sprinkly cheese'. Provided they are in the right mood they are absolutely meticulous in ensuring they each get the same quantity of cheese on their food (by that I mean 'both get more') and call out when they think someone's been short-changed.

Taking this baseline of emotional intelligence, plus their natural instinct to speak up when actions aren't fair, on explaining to them that in some situations people aren't always treated equally because of their skin colour, they are rightly outraged.

Carina from the digital collective Dope Black Mums says that teaching your children 'not to see colour' is a potentially damaging tactic. 'How will they be empathetic if they can't see the systematic oppression that occurs as a result of having a different skin tone? How will their kindness come into play if they can't see any racial biases?'[4]

So that's an introduction into explaining the problem of racial inequality. Question is, what's the action?

What can we do?

This book is focused around answering questions. To do that, I would recommend research and reflection (a.k.a. checking your assumptions).

However, acquiring knowledge and turning that into valuable conversation is only part of the equation. Eighty per cent of what children learn is through what they see in us.

Dr Beverly Daniel Tatum, author of *Can We Talk About Race?*,[5] talks about racism as 'smog'. We (both us adults and our kids) end up breathing it in, so racism ends up 'showing up in unexpected ways even when we come from families where equality was the presumed value'.

With that in mind, if we want to model fairness it needs to be apparent in how we go about our day-to-day life. It's the things our kids experience on the school run, at the supermarket or at a family get-together that count.

To be more specific, good 'actionable' starting points might include:

- Be conscious of what media and social influences you and your kids are consuming.

- Check the company you keep.

- Be mindful of what you (and in turn your children) are exposed to. What movies are you watching? What colour skin do the characters have? Who is portrayed in what ways? The same goes for the books you are reading yourself and reading them. What colour skin do their toys have? Who are you following on your social media accounts?

It's all about expanding horizons. The thought being that exposure broadens the idea of inclusiveness. Unicef explains that introducing your kids to 'diverse cultures and people from different races and ethnicities' is important because 'such positive interactions with other racial and social groups early on help decrease prejudice and encourage more cross-group friendships'.

What about fave family songs? (We've finally moved on from the *Trolls* soundtrack, thank goodness.) Music is a great way to explore other cultures. Spotify makes that easy with pre-made playlists; so get some tunes on.

Another great suggestion via Dope Black Mums is to eat food from cultures other than your own. Consuming can literally extend to what we put in our mouths and THAT is the type of education I am all over.

What better opportunity to learn about Western African culture than over jollof rice, chicken and fried plantain? (On which note, ladies, I think you offered to have me round to experience a Jamaican Sunday lunch – as soon as Covid sods off, I AM THERE!)

Be conscious of the company you keep.

Our kids learn from us, but keep in mind they are also influenced by those in our extended family or friendship circle.

Take Great Uncle John (an imaginary character for the sake of the story). Great Uncle John says the odd thing that doesn't match up to your own beliefs. While letting Great Uncle John's racist (or sexist or homophobic) words slide by for fear of rocking the boat or ruining Christmas dinner doesn't make you racist, it does run the risk of your kids thinking that racist commentary is acceptable when it's not.

So having hard but necessary conversations about race will likely mean having that chat with John too. Do it from a place of compassion and kindness. Great Uncle John needn't be someone you write off; instead try to take him from a place of ignorance to one of awareness.

Allyship is another piece of language you or your kids might come across. Allyship in this context has come to refer to being part of the anti-oppression conversation. Simplified (for kids), being an ally is shorthand for being aware and helping to make a change.

Again, sounds good but this isn't a quick-fix, one-and-done solution. Research from the Carnegie Corporation, which was summarised by the Common Destiny Alliance (CODA),[6] suggests that most of us are not as competent as we need to be in our interactions with people we perceive to be culturally different, and even people with good intentions sometimes do the wrong thing. Plus prejudice and discrimination are socially influenced.

Sadly, people cannot be inoculated against prejudice, so the teaching of fairness and actively improving equality is an ongoing commitment. One that more than likely will meet bumps in the road.

Back to the question: why has the person got different hair/eyes/skin from me?

The short answer: follicles, genes and melanin.

Longer answer: pigmentation can change how people are treated.

In an ideal world, this wouldn't be the case, so let's focus on raising the next generation to do better than that metaphorical 'Great Uncle John' did – or, indeed, than we are doing.

Drawing again on CODA's response to the Carnegie report, it flagged that 'efforts to improve intergroup relations often overstate differences among and within racial and ethnic groups, and neglect beliefs and values that are shared across racial and ethnic lines . . . [This] has the consequence of understating common human characteristics and directing attention away from the influence of gender, language, and social class on interpersonal relations.' In short, it is important to make clear that while racial and ethnic groups may have differences, they often have a lot in common.

Context is key and the 'divide' we are talking about in this instance is the difference in the way race can impact your life and the disparity racism causes. But to go back to the beginning, what *isn't* different, what we should all share, is a universal ambition to bridge the gap between Martin Luther King's dream and where we are now.

Use questions like the one we have discussed in this chapter to begin open, challenging conversations and keep them going. Continue working towards raising good humans who know to challenge prejudice and stand up for everybody's right to be treated fairly and respectfully. We need to do that by modelling these principles in our own behaviour and, crucially, being honest with ourselves when we could do better.

BUT WHY CAN'T I GO ON
THE INTERNET? *

Of the 4,000 parents I consulted for this question, a massive 83 per cent were worried about how much screen time their kids have. Some had put a blanket ban on it, only allowing it on special occasions. Others admitted to allowing upwards of five hours a day, depending on parents' workload. Personally, I have seen the screen time creep up with each of my children – Greta (my youngest) naturally got her hands on a tablet at a younger age than her siblings, simply because she learned quickly to grab them when one of the boys nipped to the loo.

Lots of parents I surveyed gave a tablet to their children when they reached the age of around three. Others introduced them at school age, while many were simply holding off as long as possible. My kids have access to a couple, but they are 'family tablets' to share rather than belonging to them specifically.

While the majority of parents in my survey gave a mobile at age eleven to coincide with their child going to secondary school, most opted for a basic phone at that point, holding off from a smart phone for as long as possible.

---

* Internet could also mean tablet, YouTube, a specific game, even borrowing your phone.

Questions I ask myself when thinking about my kids' screen time:

- How and why are they using a device? Or, more specifically, how and why am I letting them be on a screen?

- Is it useful, entertaining or necessary?

But it's a mistake to think that all screen time is bad. My boys love following drawing tutorials on there, which I love; Minecraft has been a social activity; and watching a movie on a car journey is a total lifeline.

Also, you gotta do what you gotta do. There are some occasions when you've just got to get stuff done (those newborn days, for example) and if a screen can enable that, then that is okay.

But be honest with yourself. Are you dishing out the screen to keep them quiet for the sake of keeping them quiet? If so, how long and how often are you doing this? That's where that niggly bit of self-doubt is useful. Time to rein it in.

Watch and learn from their mood. I don't know about you but I can feel when I am in a scroll hole. Gritted jaw, low mood – even some anger. I see it in the kids too – the first sign of elbowing siblings or growling at the screen, take it away.

It's very easy to fill a void of 'there's nothing to do' with a screen. But I really believe a bit of boredom is good. Provided I have the guts to ignore the moaning, I find that those are the times when they actually have to think of something to do and that's when creative ideas occur.

Stop the screens being visible. Sounds obvious. But sometimes mine think they want them because they are there. Popping them away curtails that reflex.

I have a 'no phone after 9 p.m.' rule for myself, because I know it helps me sleep better. Yet on occasion my kids' screen time creeps up so close to their bedtime that inevitably they are hard to settle (and they suddenly have a million 'but why?' questions streaming from their whirring minds).

According to internetmatters.org, for under fives it's never too early to set boundaries about when and how long your child can be on devices. Have passwords on devices. Be sure to set the homescreen to something child-friendly.

For primary school age (up until approximately the age of eleven), the focus should be on establishing positive behaviour and teaching your child to stay safe.

They suggest that rather than imposing boundaries, agree them. Similarly, the best way to know what your kid is up to online is to do it together; five minutes looking over their shoulder is a very real reminder of quite how well kids can make their way round devices and apps. For example, I naïvely told myself that mine couldn't get into too much trouble because they weren't able to spell what they were searching for, only to discover that they were just using Siri. Of course they were! Lastly, games, apps and social networks all come with an age rating – definitely worth checking.

The American social psychologist Jonathan Haidt, on the documentary *The Social Dilemma*, gave three great bits of advice that should be applied to kids (especially as they head towards their teens):

- No phones in the bedroom.

- No public social media until age sixteen.

- Decide on a 'time budget' for devices.

Mindful and measured internet use is something we should all be thinking about. Screens are useful and liberating, but they can easily creep into all aspects of our life and in turn our children's lives. We need to ensure our kids take an active, present part in the real world beyond their devices.

How about playing them at their own game with some internet-based distraction?

Here are some facts that might distract them (briefly) from their screens. And, in the interest of transparency, these facts are just from random places on the internet. Believe them if you like.

- Of all the traffic on the internet, 51.8 per cent is from bots while 48.2 per cent is from humans.

- 300 hours of YouTube video are uploaded every minute.

- The average person now spends almost ten hours a day online – we spend more time on the internet than we do sleeping!

- Google processes 5 *billion* questions a day.

This is a whole new mind-boggling world and we are learning on the fly, both with our own internet consumption and with our kids'. Our parents were convinced MTV was the worst thing that ever happened. Their parents were worried about TV full stop. Yet the internet is here to stay and, while we continue to learn and our lifestyles evolve, we have to accept there are no hard and fast rules. Instead be mindful. We know how addictive and mind-sapping it can be, but also how liberating and educational and connective. The key, I think, is to keep checking in, pull yourself up on it and check in again.

And rule number one regarding screen use: no empty threats. If I had a pound for every time we said 'no more screen time' to our kids, only to give in after they've nagged me for twenty minutes, I'd be a rich woman. But of course it's the surest way of diminishing their respect for my boundaries and attempts at authority.

In closing, going back to the pool of research I conducted, I asked for any rules or approaches my followers have when it comes to their own children and the answers were brilliantly useful. Here's a selection:

- Tell your kids they can earn ten-minute increments of screen time for doing various household jobs. (One family referred to this as a 'when and then' approach.)

- Another allows 'one charge' a week.

- Set timers on the actual device. Or use an egg timer.

- They have to do a physical activity first.

- If they want screen time, make it educational where possible.

- Use parental control apps.

- Only at the weekends.

- Never at mealtimes.

- Set time boundaries young so they are normalised. Far easier than trying to rein it in later. (There were many different examples of time rules, including 'never more than thirty minutes at once' and 'always switch off by 6 p.m.')

- Swap screens on car journeys for a playlist.

- Avoid the narrative that screens are bad; have an open dialogue about the reality and dangers of them.

- Ensure there are 'no-screen days'.

So much good advice here. Such good advice, in fact, that I am wondering whether we adults ought to try to apply some of these rules to ourselves? After all, it's hard to enforce a healthy approach to screens if you aren't at least trying to do the same yourself.

When I was a kid, I wish I had known that . . . just because someone wasn't kind to me, it didn't mean I was a bad person.

Anna Mathur @annamathur

JOINING BIT ONE:

IN SEARCH OF SILENCE

The quieter you become, the more you are able to hear.
                                                    Rumi

I have been deeply inspired by the Norwegian explorer Erling Kagge, who spent fifty days walking across the Antarctic. As if that wasn't mad enough, he also made the last-minute decision to leave the batteries to his radio in the plane. Why? As well as the physical challenge, Kagge was interested in the concept of fifty days of silence.

FIFTY DAYS OF SILENCE.

The concept of that blows my mind.

And also freaks me out.

How would I fare with nothing but my own thoughts for that long? I am genuinely not sure I could cope.

But setting aside the extreme version, Kagge argues for the importance of silence because it is within silence that we have time to think, muse, contemplate. Think about when you last had a moment of actual silence. Or at least quietness? And no, being asleep doesn't count.

Trust me, as a mother of three living in London's Zone 2 I know how scarce that is.

In any given moment there are layers upon layers of sound: Power Rangers – sports commentary – dog barking – toddler demanding snacks – sirens blaring – bins being collected, etc etc. My life couldn't feel less like the snowy expanse of 'nothingness' if it tried.

But, and it's a relatively big but (cue 'Baby Got Back'), what I have been noticing is that when I do have quiet I fill it with noise: whether I am sitting on a train or on a car journey, at the hairdressers or in the queue for the post office, all the gaps for sitting with my thoughts are now plugged with an absent-minded scroll or browse of the internet. Probably to search for some irrelevant but suddenly urgently needed nugget of information like 'When was Viennetta invented?' (1982, if you are interested).

I see myself skirting round the opportunity to sit and contemplate, partly out of habit and partly because it's unfamiliar. The silent whirr of my own thoughts can be uncomfortable, even on the ten-minute train ride to London Bridge from Peckham, let alone for an entire fifty days. But I really believe we are missing a trick, and that we need to keep that quiet moment sacred even if it's brief.

I don't know about you but things can often feel very overwhelming.

During the rollercoaster of 2020, there were several moments when I specifically remember saying to myself: 'I don't know what I think.'

That feeling scared me.

It made me feel overwhelmed and a bit lost. And also a bit stupid. But actually the reason I didn't know what I thought was because at the point of not knowing, I was plugging into Unknown Other People's thoughts and ideas, which of course I welcome, but not at the expense of my own. I simply didn't have the time or space or indeed quietness to work out how I felt myself.

And it's not just me.

I have discovered that about 85 per cent of the 3,000 people I asked on Instagram are overwhelmed too. Most of us don't have time to think because we are too consumed by the to-do list, burdened by the weight of all the things we feel we 'must' do.

Imagine that as a physical burden: all the people you pass on the street each struggling to carry their load of shopping. And don't get me wrong, I am definitely guilty of putting a bag on every limb to avoid having to make multiple trips when unpacking the car. But we can't go around like that indefinitely.

Or take a minute to describe who you are.

Here's me: mother, wife, friend, sister, podcaster, blogger, Instagrammer, daughter, client, advisor, planner, chef, cuddler, personal assistant, nurse, counsellor, role model, taxi, sounding board, supposedly even a lover and good company!

IT FEELS LIKE A LOT BECAUSE IT IS A LOT.

We cannot find time to think if we continue a) trying to be all things to all people, and b) thinking there is any way on earth we can complete all the tasks we need to do.

It is not possible to do it all. And yes, phone use and overwhelm are linked. Hide your phone for an hour and I guarantee you'll be more productive.

But that mental load, or the ticker tape as my friend Steph Douglas (founder of dontbuyherflowers.com) calls it – it is not going to stop. So we have to realise that building in pauses isn't just a nice idea; it is necessary.

Going back to my shopping bag analogy. By putting down one (or, better still, all) of the bags for a minute, you are instantly able to catch your breath and your thoughts.

Maybe in that pause you spot someone on hand who could grab a bag for you. Maybe you realise that one of the bags can be left in the car until next time. If you are too busy hastily rushing from A to B with all your bags, hoping that you'll make it through without a handle breaking, then you'll never see these opportunities to lighten the load.

The answer to 'How am I going to do it all?' is finding a window to not do anything.

What's this got to do with this book? Well, how can we hope to have the ability to fully engage our kids and their curiosity if we are burdened with the mental load? Life is noisy and busy, I get that. But what I am finally, FINALLY beginning to understand is that we can opt out of it. It's up to us.

In order to begin to answer the big questions both from our kids and from ourselves, the first thing you have to do is to create some space.

Small windows of silence. Which sounds like an impossibility when you are overwhelmed.

But here's the thing – the to-do list is never going to be completed. So instead we need to make 'giving ourselves time to think' one of the items on the to-do list.

Creating moments of silence is vital. But how?

- Activate shut-down mode on your phone. Mine times out between 9 p.m. and 7 a.m. If you can't do that, at least try leaving your phone downstairs.

- Meditate. I was very resistant to the idea of meditation. I tried it here and there but was never very good at it – rather than successfully zone out, I became preoccupied with the fact that I wasn't successfully zoning out. And so I would always give up. But then over time, enough people I respected, people who seemed to have time for self-analysis, who appeared to be wrangling busy minds, told me that meditation was a game-changer for them. So I committed to Deepak Chopra's twenty-one-day course and now, six months in, it really is one of my (near) daily habits. Disappointingly, I haven't magically reached some kind of enlightenment. But I do now feel a sense of relief when I plug into that moment of doing nothing for ten minutes every day. Mad that it feels like a luxury.

- Take a bath.
- Go for a walk.

Do things that allow you to check out. Let your mind wander. You might have some big answers, or in my case realise you don't need to go to the shop to get stuff for dinner, as your subconscious has remembered that there is a shepherd's pie in the freezer. And thus that silence, that pause, has taken 'get something for dinner' off the to-do list too.

As an aside . . . Perhaps the reason kids have so many questions is because they have time to think? And the way we can answer them properly is by giving ourselves the space (and on occasion even silence) to think about our answers.

Fi and Jane on my favourite podcast *Fortunately* talk about 'giving in to it' when your house and your brain are a mess. Trying to fight it sometimes makes things harder.

In Japanese culture they value thinking about nothing at all so much that they actually give it a name: *boketto*. Which translates as 'gazing vacantly into the distance without really thinking about anything specific'.

Sign me up for more of that, please. I'm not convinced I would do well with fifty days of silence. But that doesn't mean I can't learn to metaphorically take the batteries out once in a while.

One of the learnings I acquired from Mother of All Lists was thanks to Zoe Blaskey (@motherkind_zoe), who offers a great example of why sometimes our own self-imposed standards can end up tripping us up. Or in relation to what we have been talking about, our own self-imposed standards of trying to achieve everything, all the time, actually end up stopping us thinking straight and make answering queries from our kids seem like an impossibly tall order. Here's an extract:[7]

- I've learned that self-kindness often isn't the easy thing.

- Sometimes the hardest thing in the world is sticking to my promise to be kind to myself no matter what.

- Refusing to let guilt consume me.

- Resting without the weight on my chest of what I 'should' be doing.

- Saying 'no' when the people-pleaser in me screams at me to say 'yes'.

- Letting go of control, perfection and how I think things 'should' be.

- Constantly challenging my thoughts about myself.

- It's a daily practice that I'm committed to.

- Even more so now I'm a mum, as when I'm kind to myself I'm a much better parent.

- Setting and holding boundaries is still a work in progress for me.

- But today I know I'm doing the best I can.

- I'm more than kind to myself today, I think I actually *love* myself (still feels odd writing that).

- I see so many of us mums being so unkind to ourselves.

- Pushing harder, feeling guilty, feeling unworthy, full of fear, going through the motions, stressed and overwhelmed.

- If I could, I would give every mum out there the ability to give themselves a break, to realise how perfectly imperfect we all are and how we're all just doing our best.

- If I could say one thing to you it would be to do the inner work; it's tough, but trust me it will be the best thing you ever do. Find your true self, make the tough choices, love the real you, cherish her and most of all, be kind to her.

When I was a kid, I wish I had known that . . . it's hard to find time to read, jump in the sea and climb trees when you're a grown-up, so do as much as you can now! Romantic love takes everyday work and there is no Prince Charming galloping over the horizon. All the little things you find funny about yourself are beautiful and unique and loveable.

Melissa Hemsley @melissa.hemsley

2

QUESTIONS ABOUT
THE BODY

As you will hear in due course, I have a mixed relationship with my body.

It's taken a lot for me to learn to truly love it, in fact truth be told I may not be there yet. I am at a point where I respect it and what it is capable of and this pandemic has made me acutely aware of how valuable our health is – arguably it's the most important thing.

Perhaps more than in any other section, I feel my role here is to land the biological facts – the scientific reasons why your body does what it does – and then tie that in to an empathetic take on how that can 'feel'. Puberty, periods, even keeping fit are all parts of being human. Yet so often it seems they end up fraught with emotional baggage. Wow! That's a heavy sentence! But it's true the commonplace stuff can still wind up being tricky, despite the fact that I am sure most of us hope to raise kids that are happy in their own skin. Or, should I say, kids that stay as happy in their own skin as they were as toddlers; let's try to preserve that even as they become teens and eventually adults (eeek).

BUT WHY CAN'T I LOOK LIKE EVERYONE ELSE?

This one floored me a bit. Don't know about you but I look at my kids and think they are perfect. But that doesn't help with the answer to the question. Neither does the knee-jerk reaction of: 'Why would you want to look like everyone else? You are great the way you are.' It's all very well pressing that opinion with a rational adult brain, but think back to school-age you and try to frame it from their perspective.

Of the 3,000 or so people I asked, 90 per cent said they were self-conscious about their appearance growing up.

That's a staggeringly high number.

When I pushed for more specific information, the answers covered a huge range of perceived issues:

'All of it but mostly my white skin, my ears, chubby tummy with small boobs, goofy teeth, my freckles and red hair . . . my entire body, my nose, the hair on my arms . . . too tall . . . wished I wasn't so short . . . everything – even my knuckles . . . acne and large legs . . . my weight in general . . . big lips . . . I hated looking at myself . . . I just wished I didn't look like a woman at thirteen.'

The list goes on and on and on.

I also received messages from those with other experiences of difference in relation to appearance. These included adopted kids not resembling their families, people not having a body they associate with their gender, those facing racial discrimination and ableism (all of which we'll get into in more detail in other questions).

Though this issue appears 'superficial', it can run a lot deeper. Question is, if so many of us were so busy hating on all these parts of our appearance, what was it we saw in others that we deemed so desirable? Perhaps this can shed a bit of light on what our kids mean when they say they want to 'look like everyone else'.

The answers here were just as varied. However, a pattern soon emerged: for every person who said they wanted 'bigger boobs', there was someone who wanted small ones. Same for darker skin vs lighter skin. Blue or green or brown eyes (whichever you didn't have!). More curves, fewer curves. Some were more specific: 'calf muscles so I could wear slouchy socks the way the cool girls did'. Some wanted a contradictory amalgamation: 'to be a waif with a washboard stomach' (hello, nineties).

What stuck with me was that The Most Admired Trait of All, more than any other, was (drum roll, please) 'To Be Normal'. Yup.

That's the crux of it, isn't it? Everyone is focused on wanting to be normal.

But normal doesn't exist.

And the irony is we are all wanting to look like someone else, who is in turn preoccupied with wanting to look like someone else. The quicker we can help our children understand that what makes people different from one another is what makes them brilliant, the better it will be.

Sadly, as a parent I know there is no convenient solution here. There's a school of thought that says that a big part of our beliefs comes from how our parents spoke about our appearance and their own.

However, on the flip side there are people whose parents never ever mentioned bodies, and that felt unrealistic too. If you are the only kid in the class who wears glasses or has red hair, why pretend that isn't the case?

There's also the role of outside influences in all this. Social media gets a lot of bad press and while it is undoubtedly awash with filters and clever poses to pop out your butt while shrinking your waist, it does also present an opportunity to see more types of body. I went to a primary school where I was, for a time, one of only three girls in the entire school! This was wonderful for many reasons, but not for showing the breadth of shapes and sizes humans come in. Even the manufacturers of Barbie have upped their game on this score now – go check out the range; it's a far cry from where they were at in the eighties, thank goodness.

Candy Cohen, a mother of two young girls, who has had alopecia universalis for eight years, says: 'I tell the girls regularly that we are all special and unique and it's important to love and accept everyone for who they are. It would be boring if we were all the same.' Not having hair is part of how she is, but it doesn't make a difference to who she is.

What advice would you give your younger self? These are a few words of wisdom I've collated from my followers' responses:

'Chill out, babe, bodies are just bodies . . . Be confident – that's the most attractive thing (oh and don't overpluck your eyebrows) . . . It's all nonsense, nobody looks like they do in magazines or TV . . . What makes you different is what makes you perfect . . . You don't realise how young and beautiful you are or who you are going to become . . . Your worth has bugger all to do with your weight . . . It gets easier . . . You won't believe it, but everyone else is worrying too. Go easy on yourself and stop comparing . . . You are wonderful

the way you are (even though you wouldn't believe it).' As an adult we learn to see that what once would have made us feel different is actually a benefit.

We aren't supposed to look the same.

People will remember you for your character. Don't over-compensate to your children – it's okay for them to express these worries of not being the same. So avoid saying 'don't be silly' when your kid says they are worried about being too skinny or fat. It's very real for them. Unfortunately we can't give the wisdom of our thirties to someone in their teens (or younger). But we can be consistent in how we talk about appearances. And the world is a better place if we can all embrace our differences.

Knowing that is one thing, of course, but it can be more challenging to live by it. Confidence, acceptance, time and kindness seem like the keys, all of which, err, take time.

Two more gems. First, I wanted to weave these words of wisdom in somewhere, but didn't quite know how, so here they are: 'Don't make a comment about an aspect of some-one's appearance that can't be fixed in ten minutes.'

The second one is to share an extract from one of my all-time favourite entries to Mother of All Lists. This list – from Nichola Garde, who has achondroplasia (dwarfism) – is just marvellous; definitely worth reading in full.[8] Let's just say it flipped over my ideas of what it means to be 'different' and left me with a lovely sense of optimism. Nichola's husband also has achondroplasia, and when their first daughter was born, they were 'delighted to find she had inherited the condi-tion. [We] knew how great life could be for her and, although there would be some stumbling blocks, she would find her place in the world. Eight years on and she is proving that every day.' Three years later, they discovered that Nichola was pregnant again – this time with a baby of 'average height' (i.e. no genetic condition). In this extract, she describes how she explained this difference to her youngest daughter as she grew up:

- It's important to remind our children of all the things we have the same.

- It is just one gene that is different between ourselves and our daughter. We have so many other genes that we have in common.

- From a young age, my daughter and I would have casual conversations regarding mummy being a small mummy and how she was going to be bigger than me when she was older. However, she knew she would also look like me because of our other genes; we both have brown hair and brown eyes. And she is left-handed like her daddy.

- At the time, it felt like these conversations were more for my benefit than hers; she was far more interested in playing than listening to me drone on.

- Last September, she started school and like every parent I was worried, hoping that all the life skills we had tried to encourage, such as kindness, empathy and strength, would help her navigate through the day.

- She settled in well and ran in every morning and out every afternoon smiling and happy.

- Scooting home one day, a new friend asked her, 'Why is your mummy small?' She stopped in front of me and I strained to hear her reply.

- 'My mummy, daddy and sister are small because they were born that way. I was born with long legs so I'm going to be bigger but I have brown hair and brown eyes just like my mummy,' she answered, smiling.

- The boy smiled back and then challenged her to a race on the scooters.

- Without realising it, my daughter had created awareness and shown that, like her sister, she was here to make a difference.

Woahh, this gets me every time.

Kids are smart, aren't they? We must remember that in how we talk to them. They might not always understand all the big stuff, but so often they do get the essence of it and will come back to have that knowledge built on at another time.

Because I have been blessed (cursed) with a relentlessly over-thinking mind, I will frequently say to someone, 'I've been thinking about that thing you said . . .' (and then go in for a whole new round of discussion). I'm proud to say my eldest has started to do the same! Which does give me a taste of my own medicine, in terms of him being like a dog with a bone. But I love it! The 'appearance' conversation will often re-emerge in a few guises and can be explored in all sorts of ways.

BUT WHY DO GROWNS-UP HAVE HAIR IN THEIR ARMPITS?

Pubertyyyyyyy! The ten-year-old daughter of a friend of mine recently got a spot on her chin and burst into the room and proudly announced, 'Mummy, I think I have the puberty!' Amazing!

What is there to say? Personally I wouldn't want to go back to being a teenager going through puberty again. Even for a hefty sum of money.

And while honesty is usually the best policy, it definitely doesn't apply here. 'Puberty? Oh yeah, that's the hormonal, physical, emotional horror show that happens during your teens. So strap in, kid, coz you're in for a wild ride.' Probably not what they need to hear.

Apart from listening to Alanis Morissette, wearing Kickers shoes and dousing myself in Impulse body spray, my over-riding memory of puberty was that it was confusing. Very, very confusing. In light of this, one of the best things adults can do is to make a potentially very complex time feel more normal by being simple and informative.

Brilliantly, shortly after submitting the first draft, I was chatting to my son Bertie about this book. I explained the concept, which he liked – phew! But he went on to say that it wasn't really necessary because he probably knew most of the answers already. Classic. From there I 'tested' him with a few sample questions. One of which was: 'What is puberty?'

'Easy. That's when you change from being a child into an adult.'

Nailed it.

With a little further investigation it seemed that although he understood the headline idea, he was shady on the details. Which is fine: the advice I've read suggests that it's good to keep things very basic under the age of six and then build on things from there. It's a good idea to teach them what to expect before they get there, so that none of it's a shock when the changes happen to them – or their classmates.

For example: most girls get their first period when they're twelve or thirteen years old. Puberty starts two or two and a half years before that. And some girls can get their periods as early as age eight. Boys hit the puberty milestone later – around age ten or eleven – and that includes their first ejaculation. (I shouldn't be grossed out by it, but I can't help it; I still remember the stench of the boys' changing room and that's basically what their bedrooms are going to smell like, isn't it?!)

Acne, mood changes, growth spurts, body shape, breasts, the all-important pubic hair and hormonal changes – it's all part of growing up and everyone goes through it.

BUT it's helpful to add that everyone goes through it at their own pace at a time that is right for them (even though it might not feel that way when it's happening to you). It's not just the physical appearance that changes. Statistics show shocking numbers of girls completely changing their attitudes during puberty – 49 per cent of girls felt paralysed by the fear of failure during puberty, and 47 per cent agreed that society simply rejects all girls who fail.

According to Nora Gelperin, director of sexuality education and training at Advocates for Youth, the most important thing when talking to kids about puberty is to be reassuring. Puberty brings about so many changes that it's easy for children to feel insecure and alone. There is a need for parents to offer reassurance and be available for guidance. If in doubt, it's good to picture your tween or teenage self and attempt to recall how you would have wanted to be treated. Look to explain these changes in an age-appropriate way, in a tone that both acknowledges the enormity of what they will go through, but also makes it feel normal and navigable. Easy, right?! Ha!

BUT WHY IS THERE BLOOD
IN THE TOILET?

It was my husband who had to have the first chat with my then four-year-old about periods. I had got up early to go to the gym and had accidentally forgotten to flush the toilet after emptying my menstrual cup. I would love to have been a fly on the wall for that conversation. Apparently Ben stuck to the 'bottom-line facts'. Smart guy. 'Mummy bleeds once a month when her body gets rid of eggs it doesn't need.' Not bad.

Kids often associate blood with injury or 'something bad'. Explain this isn't the case here; in fact this is perfectly normal. Every day, 800 million women and girls are doing it. What a mad thought.

The blood is a period. Or to give it its technical term, 'menstruation'. I searched far and wide for a simple, succinct explanation and it's hard to find. This is what I pieced together:

> Menstruation is when the body is capable of becoming pregnant and begins a menstrual cycle. Approximately once a month the ovaries release an egg (ovulation). The uterus prepares for pregnancy by getting thick with cells. If the egg is not fertilised then the body cleverly gets rid of the lining it has created, which comes out through the vagina as a period. Then the whole process starts again.

Consider adding some factual detail. Bleeding usually lasts for three to eight days. For most women, menstruation happens in a fairly regular, predictable pattern. The length of time from the first day of one period to the first day of the next period normally ranges from twenty-one to thirty-five days.

It can seem a bit complex, but kids are great at absorbing as much info as they need. Bodyform conducted some research and found that one key issue is that many girls felt they found out too little, too late. Most period education came about once they had been caught short with blood in their knickers.

With this in mind, the advice is to start talking about periods early. Since some girls start as young as eight, it's good to introduce the conversation in a normal way from age six or seven.

One respondent in the Bodyform research said, 'Talk to us about periods just the same way you'd explain about skincare – so we understand what's going on physically, and what we need to do.' Great advice.

The key points are:

• Periods are not something shameful.

• Make them a normal part of conversation from as young an age as possible.

• Avoid euphemisms. They tend to cause confusion.

• Periods are about more than just the bleeding part.

• Invite questions, particularly around rumours or myths your children might be hearing.

A quote that stays with me is this one from Maisie Hill's brilliant book, *Period Power*: 'When a girl's first period is acknowledged positively or celebrated as a rite of passage instead of being ignored or expressed as a negative, they are more likely to have a positive body image and to engage in healthy behaviours such as seeing a gynaecologist.'[9]

If you are female reading this, it's worthwhile thinking back to your first period.

I remember feeling it was a definite rite of passage (up there with putting on my first bra, bought from Tammy Girl, no less!). However, I quickly learned that sanitary towels should be hidden in a secret place in the bathroom or masterfully concealed up your sleeve at school. Menstruation felt shameful and not to be talked about. (Apart from by a girl in my primary school who claimed to have started her periods before anyone else and insisted on taking people to the toilets to see the sanitary towel. It was later revealed that she had actually been colouring in the towels with a felt tip! The horror! And also just a bizarre thing.)

I digress. As per my earlier point re approaching the subject like it's about washing your face or indeed wiping your bum, there is no need to hide sanitary products. Let children look at them. Let them ask questions. Explain that the tampons/cups/sanitary towels catch the blood so it doesn't go on the underwear.

Periods are about way more than just the blood part. They impact everything: appetite, mental health, sleep, how sociable you feel. For some women it results in cramps, lightheadedness or poor skin. I went through my first thirty-five years being clueless about all of this.

The impact of your cycle is varied and I appreciate not everyone wants to geek out on this stuff. Some friends love a period-related chat and see huge benefits to tracking their cycles; for others it's not such a big deal. Wherever you land is up to you (obvs) but make sure it's not seen as embarrassing and not exclusive to the domain of 'girl chat'. Any guy who lives or works with a girl will likely benefit from knowing what periods involve too.

This is all a far cry from the education I got via the book *Are You There, God? It's Me, Margaret* by Judy Blume – those images of fat sanitary towels attached to belts via hooks still haunt me! Periods are part of life. Not something to be hidden or shrouded in mystery.

That being said, is it too much to ask to be allowed to pop to the toilet alone during my period? Being open is one thing, but nobody needs a running commentary from a small child while you are trying to insert your menstrual cup!

BUT WHY CAN'T SOME PEOPLE WALK?

This is a pretty open-ended one. Some people can't walk for a variety of reasons. Could be an injury, an illness or disability.

And of course unless you know the person or people in question, then there is no way of answering correctly. This should go without saying but those I spoke to made it VERY clear that the one thing you shouldn't do is guess!

This is a slight aside, but I am dyslexic and so my head is full of weird expressions ('necessary' is 'one coffee and two sugars', i.e. one 'c' and two 's's). One sprung to mind here: 'Assume makes an ass out of u and me.' It is true!

Even deciding something is a disability is an assumption. It could be an injury. Who knows? The possible reasons why someone can't walk are vast!

But this does present the opportunity for a wider conversation about disability.

One common confusion among kids is that 'disabled' means 'in a wheelchair'. Not so. One in seven people in the world have a disability, many of which can be hidden.

Looking for a straightforward explanation, I found the way Kids Britannica[10] framed things really helpful, explaining that disability can be a 'physical or mental' issue that in turn makes it 'difficult or impossible' for a person to do some necessary or important things. They add that some disabilities are temporary, while others 'last forever'. Sometimes a person develops a disability while in other instances they are born with it.

To get some great insight and advice on the subject I tapped up a few people. Sally Darby has multiple sclerosis and a severe visual impairment. She is the founder of Mums Like Us, a network for disabled mothers which can be found on Facebook, on Instagram @mums_like_us and at www.mumslikeus.org. Julie Seal is a disabled and chronically ill mum. Julie and I worked together at Facebook as creative strategists; you can find her @the_chronicoptimist. Priya Kaur Smith is the founder of loveDIS (@lvdisldn), a site celebrating diversity and disability. Ben Tansley was left paralysed after a motorbike accident. Martine Monksfield wrote to me about her experience of being deaf. All are parents. Each have their own experience of disability.

Taking the question in hand as a starting point, Sally shared this frank observation: 'When you have a visible disability, it's hard to ignore the range of reactions you get from strangers. There are unwelcome comments, personal questions and persistent staring eyes. On the less offensive end of the scale, but still somewhat off-putting, are the sideways glances, sympathetic head tilts or very deliberate looking the other way. These reactions happen because we have all grown up in a world that views disability as other, as a "shame", and as something you just don't talk about.'

This might be uncomfortable reading (though far less uncomfortable than being on the receiving end, I might add!), but also nods to the fact that perhaps a disability isn't a negative. 'Fact is,' says Julie, 'nobody needs to feel sorry for disabled kids or adults; many disabled people wouldn't actually want their disability to go away. They are fine with it! And many disabled people are happier than non-disabled people anyway because they've learned to be very tolerant as the world can be a trickier place when you are disabled.'

Martine Monksfield, who is deaf, said: 'If someone offered me a pill to wake up tomorrow as a hearing person, I would take that pill, crush it and blow it to the wind. I am sure some deaf people (especially those who go deaf later in life) would grab this, but not me. I am a proud deaf mum who experiences life differently. It has given me many opportunities I would not have had if I was hearing.'

On the @loveDIS Instagram page, I spotted a quote from Shani Dhanda: 'I'm only disabled when I experience barriers or bias.' The rest of the time a person is just a person; we all have challenges and success and ups and downs.

On the idea of barriers, there is a call nowadays to steer clear of the outdated narrative of 'disabled people can do anything'. In theory that might be true, but it's forgetting that until everything is fully accessible, then there are unfortunately hurdles to overcome.

Instead, think of it like this, says Julie. 'Different is kinda cool. Sure, a disabled kid might use a wheelchair or look different or not be able to do all the same things . . . but who wants to be the same as everyone else anyway? Same is a bit boring; different means more interesting, unique and often pretty cool. (Plus many disabled kids get cool things like wheelchairs to ride in, honestly lots of fun!)'

She goes on to add that 'disabled kids are pretty normal too. A disabled kid might be deaf or blind, for example, but they probably like the same TV show you do . . . or football team, or cartoon characters, or games. In fact, you are probably more similar than you realise. So don't be afraid of differences; instead find the similarities. Move away from seeing having a disability as a shorthand for being an inspiration. Sure, there are people who do amazing things, but that's a comment on them as people – not as "disabled people".'

All that being said, Sally says she still sees a level of embarrassment and awkwardness among many parents when it comes to talking about disability with their children.

What's the solution?

For Sally, it's clear: 'Young children are inquisitive. Their thoughts and perceptions are malleable. We know all too well how our behaviours and opinions can influence them. If we duck our heads to avoid the eyeline of a disabled person, our children will do the same, and the cycle will continue.' (She is keen to add that this is just her experience and therefore she can't speak for all disabled people. She is also speaking as somebody who was not disabled until 2008 when the early symptoms of multiple sclerosis hit. So she can see this issue from all sides.)

'We must be honest with our children,' Sally continues. 'Don't shhh them. Don't tell them it's rude to stare or point. Don't tell them you'll talk about it later then try to sweep it under the carpet. Talk to them, openly and honestly.

'Tell them all bodies are different.

'Tell them some bodies are very small, while others are very tall.

'Tell them some people learn in different ways to them and others move in different ways.

'Tell them that every body is unique and brilliant in its own way.

'Teach them that disability is not something to fear or be confused by, nor is it something to laugh at or mock.

'Teach them that every person deserves our respect and kindness and that every person deserves dignity. "Disabled" is a neutral word, like "blonde" or "tall". When they learn this, they will not stare or point because they will know, from what you have shown them through your example and words, that that person is just another human, getting on with their day.'

A recurrent theme when looking to answer the questions in this book is that parents are worried about saying the wrong thing or causing offence. Sally totally gets that. 'I would much rather hear a parent say to their child, "I don't know why she has a stick but we don't need to know why. Everybody is different and isn't that wonderful?" as opposed to, "Shhh, don't be rude,"' says Sally, before going on to share a story.

'Recently a friend of mine's daughter asked me, "Why do you walk like that, Sally?" How refreshing! I explained to her that I have a health condition called multiple sclerosis. It affects the way I move and means I can't see very well. This was more than enough information for the seven-year-old girl, who skipped away and told her mum, "Did you know Sally has a multiple something?"'

To reiterate the point at the beginning of this question: the one thing we absolutely must not do is feed them misinformation.

Don't speculate or guess as to the cause of someone's disability. Just say, 'It's not important.' If you don't know, you don't need to make something up. Hearing that from Sally, I wanted to laugh at the awkward absurdity of someone plucking something from thin air. However, one thing we know for sure is that when we feel the pressure, people panic and say and do weird things.

Says Sally: 'Be honest. Tell your child you don't know why, just as we don't know why you have big feet or I have brown eyes or why our neighbour has a scar on his elbow. We don't need to know everything.' Yup, yup, yup.

Be conscious of language. Julie says, 'The word "disabled" is absolutely okay to use, but everyone has their own preferred language to describe themselves too. For example, someone

I know with a condition that means she can't control her muscles calls herself "wobbly", not disabled. It's sometimes a good idea to ask a friend how they would like you to refer to their "thing".'

And a big red flag from Julie: look out for using the word 'wrong', e.g. 'that person has X wrong with them'. The implications of that are damaging, as is the idea of disability as any kind of 'other'.

The question in hand refers to a visible disability. But there are many people who have invisible or 'chronic' (that means long-term) illnesses that make them less able to do stuff. Julie, who herself has chronic illness, says, 'They might look very "normal" but be less able to walk around or play or take part in fun activities. It's not that they don't want to play, it's that their bodies don't work in the same way; often their cells don't make enough energy or they have lots of pain. So that can mean it's hard to do "normal" stuff. But it's important to remember that they can still enjoy calmer, quieter things, maybe things they can do together, like watching films, reading or making art. So it's nice to be understanding of adults or kids who can't do the "energy" activities but are better doing the calmer things instead. And not to make them feel bad that they can't take part, but instead include them in the calm stuff.'

Ben Tansley, who was left paralysed after a motorbike accident, also touches on the unseen nature of disability and how actually the bits people assume to be the problematic part are often minor compared to the struggles that happen behind closed doors. For him, the most important thing to point out is: 'It doesn't make us any different. Physically I changed, but I was still me and still as happy as ever. I think sometimes people are too quick to judge that you should actually be depressed.' It's such an important point. Never patronise.

Never assume. Remember that every disability is different. Always take people individually.

And one last important nugget from Sally. She believes that as our children get older, we should be teaching them about the prejudices and discrimination disabled people have faced, so they know that 'it has been really bad, but that progress is being made and that they are part of it. Their non-judgement and inclusivity will see them working alongside disabled people in diverse boardrooms and organisations. It's a future that sees disabled people as equal to their non-disabled peers and starts to design a world that meets their access needs and requirements. It's been a long time coming and it's in their hands.'

While there is no one answer here and no two people have the same lived experience (that would be very freaky), what might be similar is the barriers they have come up against. For example, don't be sorry that someone isn't walking; be sorry that the London Underground is inaccessible.

It's not a disabled person's job to make able-bodied people feel comfortable with their disability. It is all of our responsibility to make the world more accessible and inclusive.

BUT WHY DON'T BOYS
WEAR DRESSES?

Short answer: boys do wear dresses.

Long answer: some facts for you. In Victorian England it was commonplace for boys and girls to wear dresses, up until they were seven. Outside Western cultures, men's clothing commonly includes skirts and skirt-like garments.

Think kilts in Scotland. Or in Myanmar, guys rock a paschou, which is 2 metres long and 0.8 metres wide – sounds hard to navigate! The word *thawb* is the standard Arabic word for 'garment' and is actually a long robe worn by men. Then there's the sulu, which is a kilt-like garment worn by men and women in Fiji since the nineteenth century. Official uniform sulus, worn by the military and the police, come to below the knees and feature a distinctive zigzag hem.

While in the West, boys and men commonly wear trousers, personally I employ the 'anyone can wear anything' approach to things.

It's probably off the point slightly, but hey, humour me. I vividly remember a holiday in the south of France when I was a teenager where my brother was allowed to wear Dr. Martens to dinner and I wasn't. I wanted to pair them with a patchwork floaty dress – channelling my inner 'Blossom' but without the kooky hat with the turn-up. Not only was I devastated not to be able to wear what felt like an excellent outfit, it was the injustice of one rule for one and one rule for the other that stung. Which of course made me want to wear those DMs even more.

It took me until my mid-thirties to realise I could go to black-tie events (this was when I was still in advertising where awards dos were commonplace) and not wear a dress! The first time I showed up in a suit I felt badass: warm and comfortable and like me. On another day I might opt for a dress because dresses are also good. But the realisation that the rules about what to wear were actually imaginary was amazingly liberating.

More things to ponder when you are dealing with questions about clothes:

- Wear the clothes that you feel like 'you' in.

- Better still, wear the clothes you feel the best in.

- Get away from chasing that 'new clothes feeling'. The idea that you need to get new stuff for the sake of new stuff needs to stop.

- Buy clothes that you love at the highest price you can afford. Wear them again and again.

- Kids are amazing at finding something they love and wearing it over and over. There's a lot to learn from that, and it's way better for the environment.

- Clothes can be fun.

- Anyone can wear anything, though ideally it should be practical.

- As long as you are respectful of the situation you're in – don't wear football kit at a wedding, for example – then go for your life.

Aside from having a discussion with your child about what clothes we can wear, it might be that as a parent you are wondering whether questions like these play into a wider conversation about gender identity, which for me begins with the basics of understanding and being able to explain the difference between 'biological sex' and 'gender'.

Sex refers to a person's sexual anatomy, their chromosomes, hormones, and internal and external sex organs. The terms 'male' and 'female' are often used to talk about an individual's sex.

Gender refers to behaviours and characteristics that society tends to associate with males and females or are termed 'masculine' or 'feminine'. There are no definitive versions of this, but these ones come up often (including in Unicef's Voices of Youth blog[11]).

Traits that are considered 'masculine':

- Dominant
- Strong
- Independent
- Decisive
- Assertive
- Brave
- Logical

Traits that are considered 'feminine':

- Collaborative
- Emotional
- Nurturing
- Flexible
- Vulnerable
- Caring
- Intuitive

Continuing the conversation further, you might talk about some of the following issues.

Gender identity is how someone feels inside. That could be 'like a boy' or 'like a girl' or perhaps 'both' or 'neither of the above'. Also, in my case at least, it's hard to know what gender I feel like inside; I feel like me and don't have anything to compare it to.

Gender expression is how people show the world their gender (the frilly dress, the swagger, the long princess hair, the bow tie). Think Harry Styles wearing a tuxedo-dress hybrid on the front cover of *Vogue*. The feminist illustrator Florence Given waxed lyrical to me about enjoying the theatre of gender expression, in terms of make-up and clothes.

Sometimes biological sex, gender and gender identity fit neatly together, but sometimes the person doesn't feel like those parts of them match up. That shows up in a few ways:

Intersex: Susannah Temko was a colleague of mine at Facebook, who later gave an amazing TED Talk on her experience as an intersex woman.[12] I then had the opportunity to interview her about it for *Honestly*. She explained: 'Intersex refers to people who are born with variations in their sex characteristics. So that's your hormones, your chromosomes, your genitals – reproductive organs that don't fit within the typical binary definitions of male and female.' We have been told that 'there are just two categories when it comes to human: there's male, there's female, and it's very set. It's just not true.' Although it's hard to give exact figures, Susie tells me that the UN agrees that 1.7 per cent of the population is intersex, which for reference is approximately the same as the percentage of people with naturally red hair.

Transgender: this means you identify with a different gender from the one you were assigned at birth. Trans activist Charlie Craggs explains: 'Some boys don't feel comfortable as a boy –

they feel in their heart like they were born in the wrong body and should have been born a girl (and vice versa). I was like this when I was little and would tell my mum I wished I was a girl. Words like "boys" and "girls" are just labels and we should be kind to everybody whether they are a boy, a girl, a boy who feels like a girl or a girl who feels like a boy. It doesn't matter what's inbetween our legs. It matters what's in our hearts. Be kind to everyone even if they're different to you.'

The conversation about trans and whether, when and how medicine should intervene with a child who is expressing issues with their gender is a complex one (and one that I can't adequately cover in this book). Speaking to one doctor who works at a well-known clinic, he felt the most-needed resource for any child and their family was time and support, not to necessarily deter them from making life-changing decisions but to ensure they were doing so with their eyes wide open.

From the reading I have done, it appears that experts, including plannedparenthood.org, agree trans and gender-nonconforming kids are consistent, insistent and persistent. More specifically, they feel strongly about their identity. They don't go back and forth; instead they clearly identify with one specific gender identity, over an extended period of time.[13] This is a useful guide to refer back to.

In the meantime, to go back to the question of whether boys can wear dresses, Charlie's advice mirrored mine: 'Boys and girls can wear anything they like; clothes are just pieces of fabric, but some silly adults make rules about clothes because they are mean and have nothing better to do with their time. You should wear whatever makes you feel comfortable – if you are a boy who likes to wear dresses that's okay and if you're a girl who likes to wear trousers that's okay too.'

And in terms of the big picture conversation about gender, this is ever-changing.

To quote *National Geographic*: 'The conversation continues, with evolving notions about what it means to be a woman or a man and the meanings of transgender, cisgender, gender nonconforming, genderqueer, agender, or any of the more than fifty terms Facebook offers users for their profiles. At the same time, scientists are uncovering new complexities in the biological understanding of sex.'[14]

Generally speaking, kids are way more open than adults. New experiences and situations are the norm for them. Thus each generation makes shifts in areas such as this. It is also worth noting that none of the above stands in opposition to kids who display what are considered more traditional gendered traits either. We are here for it all: boyish boys, girlie girls, boys who are girlie, girls who are boyish and everything in between that maybe we can't even adequately put into words (did I mention the floral dress/DM boot situ? Oh yeah I did, I'll get over it soon).

Keep things neutral. Keep talking. And forget dresses on boys – why on earth is it that toddlers insist on wearing wellies on the hottest day of the year, but want nothing but sandals in the snow? Answer me that!

When I was a kid, I wish I had known that . . . it's okay to feel different from all the other boys. There are girls like me who are born in the wrong body and one day I'll get to be the girl I never got to be when I was a kid.

Charlie Craggs @charlie_craggs

BUT WHY DO PEOPLE
EXERCISE ANYWAY?

Short answer: for me it's simple. I exercise because it makes my head and body feel good.

Long answer: it hasn't always been that way. If you wouldn't mind indulging me for a moment, here's a summation of my experience of exercise, from being 'the kid picked last for PE' to – much to my surprise – becoming someone who loves fitness.

It's a hot July day, the sun is on my back, there is grass up my nose and the murmur of encouraging cheering in the background. I've fallen flat on my face during the sack race. Of course I have! I was always the kid picked last for PE. The kid who was awarded some kind of made-up prize for 'enthusiasm'. I don't know whether I decided I wasn't a sporty kid or it was decided for me. I was creative, and back then you were either a 'drama sort' or a 'sports sort'.

Exercise was pretty non-existent until around the end of school/beginning of university when I realised that going to the gym could make you lose weight. For the following years, exercise specifically in the pursuit of burning calories was part of my life. Which sounds good on the one hand – raising your heart rate is a positive – but my motivation was out of whack. I'd spend what felt like hours on a running machine telling myself how much I hated my body. I was absolutely convinced that if I could shrink down and achieve a mythical 'beach body' then it would make all my other issues disappear.

What's really maddening is that I should have known better. I knew that there was airbrushing going on in magazines; I knew that no one could live on cabbage soup forever and that sticking electronic pads to your tummy wasn't going to miraculously give you a six-pack. I knew all that and I still got suckered in. FOR YEARS.

So that was my relationship with exercise up until my mid-thirties: I had shifted from a non-participant to someone who did it solely out of joyless obligation.

That was until two years ago when I stepped into my local CrossFit gym. I was five months postpartum with my third child. During their 'Strong as a Mother' class they offered a baby-holding service while mums trained. Sounded like a dream; even if I didn't enjoy the exercise, at least I could have a window of me-time.

My ambitions were also realistic. Given that this was my third baby I had learned there was no such thing as 'snapping back'. My body tends to hold on to baby weight for as long as I breastfeed and I was okay with that. Crucially, it meant I wasn't showing up to those classes with the hope of getting into my old jeans. Quite the opposite: because Greta was my last kid, I was determined to enjoy those elasticated waistbands for as long as possible.

This meant my motivation for going to the gym was, for the first time ever, to do with my head, not my body. I wasn't fixated on physical results; I was there because of how it made me feel. I soon learned that working up a sweat was a sure-fire way to shift my mood. However tired and hormonal I was, if I could just drag myself through the door at The Yard then the outcome would be positive. No matter what, I always left feeling better than when I arrived. And that is powerful.

It didn't stop there. Once you frame exercise as an act of self-love (as Bryony Gordon puts it) rather than punishment, then suddenly it becomes something you *want* to do, rather than *have* to do.

Throughout school and uni, I never trusted those 'sporty types'. Why on earth would they *choose* to spend their Saturdays playing sport? When they could have been doing, well, anything else? Now I get it. In fact, I feel sad that I missed out on all those years.

Nice ramble, Telford, but what's your point?

Good question. PE, particularly if you have a terrible experience of it, is a pivotal moment. According to the Youth Sport Trust, the biggest drop-off from participation in sport occurs during the transition from primary to secondary school, with disruption to friendship groups and declining body confidence among the main reasons cited for the decline. I can totally relate. PE soon became *the* worst part of my week, which is saying something given that it was pitched against double maths. This was partly because I had to wear gym knickers. Cruel, cruel, cruel. Nobody feels their best self in gym knickers. I joke: in truth it goes deeper than that.

Of the 3,000 people I surveyed, only 37 per cent enjoyed PE at school. When I pushed for the reason why, answers included:

'PE focused solely on performance not on how it made you feel . . . It only ever focused on the people who were good at it . . . I felt awkward and conscious of my body . . . The competitive element sucks if you are the one who is last all the time . . . Hated the aspect of being watched by the rest of the class . . . Lack of choice . . . Having to shower naked with everyone afterwards . . . Uninspiring teachers . . . It was always so cold – I always associate it with being absolutely freezing.'

Insightful. None of this is a great introduction to exercise or a great way of teaching the joy of movement to children.

Common problems seem to be:

- Lack of variety
- Too much focus on competitive sport
- Lack of self-confidence
- Lack of positive encouragement

Youth Sport Trust findings state that 'pressure of school work and low confidence are much bigger barriers to taking part in physical activity for girls than boys' (24 per cent of girls compared to 13 per cent of boys).

Furthermore, they have discovered that satisfaction with body image for girls declines with age. One in four are unhappy with their body image at eleven to thirteen years and this figure increases to one in three by the time they reach fourteen to sixteen years. And, crucially, 'girls do not see the relevance of the skills they learn in PE to their lives' (45 per cent of girls compared to 60 per cent of boys).

How do we improve the prospect of keeping kids moving (and enjoying it)? One person said the best way to improve PE was to not do it! I see where they are coming from, but hopefully there are some other ways to solve the problem.

The overwhelming feedback I had from my respondents was that more variety in terms of activities offered, less focus on sport and competition, and more purposeful encouragement would all help kids relate to PE more.

This led me to two thoughts.

Firstly, from what I understand, PE in schools has shifted significantly. At the very least there are no more gym knickers. So there is hope that things are slowly changing. And secondly, there is a role for the family in this.

On which subject, I was interested to catch up with a family friend who wrote a post on Facebook that brought a ton of interesting points to the topic. Emily Yirrell is head of Personal, Social, Health and Economic education (PSHE) at a middle school, as well as being a PE and science teacher and a mum of three, so she has a good insight into the subject. She recommends doing the following things with your children:

- Do exercise/activity together; go for walks and bike rides as a family. Talk about how this makes you feel afterwards and why being active is so good for our brains, body and mind.

- Find an exercise/activity you enjoy; it doesn't all have to be about lifting weights or running. If you enjoy it, you will maintain it.

- Talk about how activity/exercise helps to keep our heart healthy, and our lungs, bones and muscles strong.

I would add to that:

- Do your children see you moving? And talking positively about it?

- Consider making that movement joyful: walk along a log, have a go at kicking that football back, or dance in the kitchen.

- This is not just for mums/daughters. Plenty of people messaged me about sons wanting to consume protein shakes like their dads or be shredded like their idols. It's good to discuss and model the idea that healthy exercise is about how you *feel*, not just about how you look.

- I really believe there is a type of exercise for everybody and that doesn't mean you have to be good at it. All you have to do is to enjoy it, or – more importantly – to enjoy how it makes you feel afterwards. Celebrate the joy of 'having a go'.

One piece of research that I come back to time and time again is this (again by Sport England): young people aged eleven to fifteen with an active mother are more likely to be active, compared with young people with an inactive mother. So working out turns out to be beneficial to you AND potentially to your kids too. Sounds like a win-win to me.

As well as role modelling, exercise can also make you a better parent. I spoke to Joe Wicks for an episode of *Honestly*. Joe – a.k.a. The Body Coach, a.k.a. the man who became the nation's PE teacher during lockdown, getting an astonishing 70 million people moving, and also father of two young kids – reiterates the importance of prioritising your own movement and finding half an hour away for yourself. 'If I'm stressed or I've got a busy day . . . I go and work out and I come down and I'm a different man. I'm a better dad, I'm kinder to Rosie, I'm more patient with Indie and Marley. So you're doing them a good thing by looking after your mindset. Your health and your mindset are so important.'

I totally agree. For me it shows up with a tight jaw and being a bit short-tempered, but if I go and do a workout I come back buzzing. Well, I mean, your kids would always opt to lose you for twenty minutes to come back being the better version of you, rather than to have you hang around being a misery, right?

But I wanted to get an idea of the reality. Back to my faithful surveys.

Of those adults who had previously disliked PE at school, 58 per cent liked it in adulthood. Not surprisingly, many said that the route to that was being able to experiment and finding something that they enjoyed and worked for them. Some said they only enjoyed Pilates or weight-training. That's the point. You don't have to like all things. You just have to find the ones you do like.

Of those who still didn't exercise, energy, time and inclination seemed to be the biggest barriers to entry. Totally relatable.

There is no quick-fix answer here. For me this is about breaking the cycle. The less I move, the less I want to move. The mind has a great way of tricking you into doing things that aren't healthy for you (more chocolate, another glass of wine, that extra episode on Netflix).

This is especially true if, as for many of us, exercise is associated with gym knickers in the cold, or hours spent working up a sweat in the pursuit of being smaller. How has exercise come to be seen as a sort of purgatory in which an infinite time must be spent on a machine as punishment?

There is another way. Exercise can be a celebration of what your body can do. *It can just be movement for the sake of movement.* The way you feel afterwards is extraordinary. More importantly, we mustn't lose sight of the fact that exercise isn't just 'a nice idea'. Our bodies are made to move. Moving increases life expectancy and quality of life. Which is why I feel so passionately about it.

I understand how it feels to be the person on the sidelines or the one who feels as if they will forever be metaphorically 'picked last'. I know how much confidence it takes to get moving when your bits are jiggling, but I also know that if you can just have a go, the gains (and not in the gym-bro's sense) are worth it.

The important part is to keep going. I don't mean keep going at something you hate: keep going until you find something you love. Street dance, mountain biking, judo or trampolining – there really is something for everyone.

Whether you are in your teens, twenties or even seventies, please don't count yourself out; instead keep trying as many ways as possible to break a sweat until you find the thing that makes your head and heart feel good. And then keep doing it. Every time you raise your heart rate or stretch a muscle, you aren't just keeping yourself well for your kids, you are increasing the chances that they'll do the same for themselves.

Conclusions:

Interestingly, when navigating tricky questions around the body, kids already have the answers. Though they might not be able to explain the ins and outs of a menstrual cycle, they are blessed with an innate connection to their own bodies. Have you ever seen a kid squat? Arse to grass with zero effort. They also intuitively understand their own appetite. They have a natural confidence – naked dancing, anyone? Similarly, they don't judge physical difference in others. They may be curious about them, but it is adults who project preconceived and potentially harmful views.

Whether we mean to or not, it is we adults who make an issue of anything to do with the body. So the real work that needs to be done when answering questions is to look at our own relationship with the subject.

All bodies are different. And that's what makes them so brilliant.

Not only that but they are changeable too; most notably for kids, puberty can change their bodies dramatically so conversation needs to be fluid. But also there is room for fun. I received an email from a mother whose daughter wanted to know 'when she would get to have a beard on her fanny'. Which is excellent. It doesn't need to become heavy. In fact, I'm giggling writing it.

If in doubt, go for 'science and kindness'. Give them some facts, but also acknowledge that bodies are weird and wonderful and that's okay.

JOINING BIT TWO:

THE ART OF CONVERSATION
(AND LISTENING)

*When you talk, you are only repeating
what you already know. But if you listen,
you may learn something new.*

Dalai Lama

On the podcast *This American Life*, there was a great anecdote
that stayed with me. There's a guy who has a high-pressure
job, where work often seeps into his home life. To add to the
pressure, his nine-year-old daughter suddenly develops a love
of questions. Not unusual for kids. But she really goes for it.
A barrage of questions at every opportunity.

To create some space for himself, he asks her to write down
the questions. Rosie (his daughter) comes back with an exten-
sive collection of enquiries covering the most fundamental
human questions – about fifty of them. Years and years later,
he is still getting through them. (He should have a crack at
trying to write them into a book!)

It reminds me of what I see being played out on social media.
Everyone wants to be heard but nobody wants to listen.

Giving someone your time and attention and making them
feel heard is such a powerful act. Yes, with kids, talking can
be a delay tactic to put off going to bed. But try to remember
that the act of listening to your child is often as important as
what is being said in the conversation. It shows you respect
their views.

The philosopher and author Alain de Botton also reminds us to be aware that often when a child says, 'I hate it here, I want to go home,' our reflex is to smooth it over. But we are missing a trick for both important conversations and valuable questions from that starting point.

Opportunities for conversation:

In the same way as I'm trying to make space for silence, I am attempting to be more conscious of preserving the opportunities for conversation with my kids.

- Sometimes that can be achieved by setting bedtime ten minutes earlier, so that when they ask the big questions I can focus properly (after sorting out the itchy pillow/ getting the water/finding the teddy/dicking about with the lighting, etc).

- Walk slowly to the park, rather than dragging them there because you are running late.

- Insist your child's screen is off on car journeys (okay, not the whole journey if it's a long one, I'm not mad. But part of it).

- Take your meals together and use that time to talk.

Idle chat is precious:

A snapshot from my life. It's Saturday. We have no plans at all, and we are still in PJs at 1.15 p.m. For people always on the go that is unusual. I'm cooking and Bertie is playing with his Lego.

What starts as a conversation about me asking him to try massaman curry turns into something much bigger. It goes something like this.

'Can you keep the curry and the rice separate?' Bertie says.

I chuckle and respond with: 'I have been your mummy for seven and a half years, which means what?'

'It means you know what I like.'

'But being your mummy means I also want to push you to try new stuff. So you try as much as possible. And then one day you will be the adult. And do you know what that means?'

I was expecting him to say, 'I'll get to eat plain rice all day.'

In fact he starts to say, 'I'll have children and make them eat new things.' But he catches himself and stops. 'I don't know if I will have kids, because I don't know who I'll marry,' he says instead.

And BOOM, there it is. A deep conversation that comes about because of a seemingly irrelevant chat about rice.

Filler chat for the sake of filler chat is no use to anyone. But small talk can be huge. Irrelevant discussions can actually become the important ones. Ask someone what their favourite biscuit is and you'll likely find the conversation flows to something deeper.

Check yourself on gossiping too. It's habitual, especially amongst women. And of course there is some value to be gained from reflecting on how others' experiences may be different or similar to your own. But gossip is talking about other people – and really, what do we learn from someone else's experience without them being able to share it with us? Instead what we should be doing is truly engaging with the person right in front of us to see how THEY are doing.

But as well as the small talk, go for the big chats too. In researching this book I've become that person who always has the big questions (sorry to those who have been subjected to it along the way; you know who you are). Once you start doing it, you can't stop. By asking for their thoughts on the big stuff, I have seen friends I've known for years in a new light. It's a constant reminder that everyone has something to add to a discussion.

Good conversation is something you can get better at:

I have a couple of mates who are excellent story-tellers; they can spin a yarn and hold an audience in a special kind of way. They are also good at accents, which I am doubly jealous of. But here are some ways you can improve your own conversational skills.

- My therapist taught me the phrase, 'Say more.' It's a really powerful tool to use with others.

- Don't let the awkward moments trip you up. Research by social psychologist Dr Gillian Sandstrom shows that even if conversations feel awkward, they're probably going better than you think.

- Ask fewer generic questions, like: 'How was school?' The answer is inevitably, 'Okay.' It really hit home that the kids were finding my chat dull when they told me I asked them every day what they'd had for lunch.

- If a conversation has left you with more questions, go back to it later. I love it when someone says, 'I've been thinking about that chat we had.' Even if they disagree with you, it's a compliment to inspire someone to mull.

- Pick your timing. Be wary of too many questions too soon. I don't know if it's because I'm dyslexic, but the combination of arriving in a new setting plus a stream of questions can send my brain into meltdown. Sometimes

I need a moment to acclimatise before being ready to engage in any kind of chat.

- If a conversation is hard, it's probably one worth having.

- Check your own answers. Don't default to saying you are fine if someone asks how you are. 'Fine' doesn't give someone anything to work with. If you feel excited or relieved about something, both are conversation starters. Let someone in.

Also, a note on 'vulnerability hangovers'. They are a thing – whenever I am really open with someone I can feel weird and wobbly the next day. Probably because a greater conversation requires openness, which can feel uncomfortable, especially if you are having a crack at putting your own thoughts out into the world. But go with it – don't be tricked into thinking it wasn't a great thing to do. Also I appreciate it when someone acknowledges the leap of faith. 'Thanks for opening up/ sharing your thoughts' is such a thoughtful comment, and it cements the trust.

Lastly, being able to have a conversation is what makes us human. Think of the experience of lockdown. It reminded me of the early part of parenting. That feeling of disconnection. I was so craving human contact that I began to talk to everyone I met. Even the drunk homeless person who makes the same joke every time ('Oi, love, have you got a million pounds?').

I used to be suspicious of those people who would talk to anyone. I thought it was weird. Now I get it. In a study from Elizabeth Dunn and Gillian Sandstrom,[15] a group of students were asked to carry around counters and keep count of all their social interactions over the course of their day. Having more social interactions – even with mere acquaintances – led the students to report greater levels of happiness and well-being. Both extroverts and introverts can benefit from this.

In short, the more you make conversation, the better you'll get at it and the more you'll get out of it. Don't expect conclusions, don't expect to agree, don't expect to end where you began and don't expect to always 'get' what the other person is saying. But if you don't, don't be afraid to dig deeper and to ask more.

I don't know about you but raising a kid who can hold a good conversation feels like a solid thing to aim for to me. So on that note: here is a random collection of my fave conversation starters (many of them have appeared in the opening 'quick-fire round' on my podcast, *Honestly*):

- What's your worst habit?
- How would your best mates describe you?
- Tell me all the things that make you feel safe.
- What are your top three biscuits?
- Tell me about your happy place.

Which moves me nicely on to another one of these:

When I was a kid, I wish I had known that . . .
fear is the sign that you're doing life right.

Clare Pooley @clare_pooley

3

QUESTIONS ABOUT
RELATIONSHIPS

I instinctively wanted to introduce this chapter by saying 'I am a people person'. But on reflection I am not convinced that's entirely true. Though I enjoy socialising, I am no social butterfly; my dream situation is a dinner with eight people – enough to have a really good chat with each person rather than flitting from one snippet of small talk to another. I find that exhausting and meaningless.

I may not be a social butterfly but I am fascinated by people. Some might say that it's being nosy. What I mean is that I love unearthing other people's stories. What my blog Mother of All Lists and podcasts, *Honestly* and *But Why?* have taught me, more than anything, is that everybody has a story. Everybody is going through or has experienced something huge and yet when we see them push a swing in the park or queue at the post office they look ordinary. Without wanting to sound really pukey, I do think all humans are both ordinary and remarkable.

I am rambling now, shall we crack on? Here's to learning from other people about how they relate to other people, if ya get what I mean!

BUT WHY WON'T THEY BE
MY BEST FRIEND?

Ahhhh, this takes me straight back to the playground. That gut-wrenching feeling of being left out. Of wanting to find that person to share a Forever Friends necklace with (remember them? Each BFF got one half of a heart strung on a chain).

At the time I was absolutely convinced it was only me it happened to. Much like I was certain I was the only one who didn't have jelly shoes, a shell suit or a Bluebird Toys kitchen (remember the one from the advert?). But judging by the overwhelming reaction from those I surveyed, there is clearly a lot of anxiety about friendship when it comes to our children.

This of course comes from a desire to protect our babes from the first experience of a kind of heartbreak. And it's not just us parents; teachers feel the same on being asked this question by a child in their class.

Did you have a best friend at school? Only 48 per cent of the people I asked did. Worse still, they all assumed that *everybody* else did.

So how do we go about a) answering the question, and b) moving away from this very finite 'all or nothing' approach to friendship?

Here are some pointers:

- Acknowledge that it can be upsetting. Avoid the temptation to soften the blow. It makes their very real feelings seem invalid. See the earlier point re the Forever Friends necklace – this stuff hurts when you are small!

- Consider throwing the question back at them: 'Why do you think this person won't want to be your best friend?' They might well have the answer already, they just don't know it.

- Explore the idea that actually there is no need to have just one best friend. It's so much better to have lots of best friends.

- Sometimes a simple approach is best. You could say: 'Because you weren't meant to be. You might not have found your best people yet. But give it time and you will.'

Unfortunately, there isn't an easy answer to the 'why?' question here. Even though we might want them to, the person doesn't have to give a reason if they don't want to be their best friend. And even if they do, it doesn't always make sense.

Whether we like it or not, it's important to try to get comfortable with the idea of not being liked. I am thirty-eight and have yet to achieve that. But I would be thrilled if my kids didn't fixate on editing themselves for other people. One person suggested food-based analogies here, to soften the blow. You can be the best peach going but some people don't like peaches, they like bananas. (It's beside the point, but peach skin makes my skin crawl; I'm very grateful for nectarines, their bald cousins!)

Which, while we are here, leads me to check in with some of my own hard-learned truths on friendship that I still have to remind myself of as an adult . . .

Adult lessons on friendships:

Friendships are for a reason, a season or a lifetime. Not all friendships are supposed to last. That doesn't make the friendship less valuable, it just means you have outgrown one another.

We are constantly evolving into new versions of ourselves and if it feels hard to maintain a bond with someone, it could well mean that one or the other or even both of you have simply evolved to a different place. I love this quote from an anonymous source: 'Grow as you please; if I have to meet you again I will do that.'

Though undoubtedly tough, when you feel a friend has 'moved away' (I am thinking metaphorically, but it could be physically), there's something helpful in framing it as a 'see you later', rather than a goodbye.

As I get older, I am enjoying seeing people coming back into my life; there's something particularly sacred about a friendship that grows back together.

That said, I don't know about you but one of the positive but surprising outcomes of the Covid pandemic is that my friendship circle has shrunk. This was not so much a conscious decision, more that everyone's capacity is limited. And that's okay. We can't be there for everyone all the time, especially in a year like 2020. Better to focus on being a great friend to a few people, than an average one to many.

Also, we are not 'supposed' to know what someone we knew when we were sixteen and three-quarters is up to. That FOMO about not being invited to something or not still being connected is utterly fabricated by social media. Try, if you can, not to pay attention to that gut feeling it triggers (probably because it reminds you of what you felt in the playground).

Lastly, if a friendship leaves you feeling rubbish then allow it to dissolve.

Great friends call you out on stuff and they have honest conversations with you, but they should also have your back and make you feel valued – otherwise they don't deserve you. If you wouldn't want that kind of friendship for your kid, don't allow it for yourself.

Final thought:

I read somewhere that a best friend isn't a person, it's a tier. (Although Covid/2020 has made 'tier' one of the words I now shudder on hearing – that and 'bubble'!) I love this positive framing and would definitely look to weave it into my answer to any question about friendship. Perhaps I would give examples of all my top-tier people and explain why I love them and the type of stuff I like doing with them: some friends like talking about tricky subjects, some like to do workouts with me, for example. They are all great and I wouldn't pick a favourite because they are all my favourites.

BUT WHY ISN'T MY FAMILY LIKE EVERYONE ELSE'S?

This is reminiscent of the 'why can't I look like everyone else?' question. That craving to be 'average' is strong, isn't it? The reality is, the idea that 'everyone else' has the same sort of family is imaginary.

But how to explain it? Families come in all shapes and sizes. And that is probably enough of an answer in itself.

Consider trying to unpack what lies behind the question: what are they really asking? Are they comparing themselves to another family they know? What is it that is appealing about the other family? Can you talk through the similarities and differences between their own situation and that of other children that they know? Can you even make it into a game? It's quite fun depicting families that you know and love and creating a very visual demonstration that, indeed, families do come in all shapes and sizes.

Think about what family actually means. Personally, I have the family who I share a home with. I have an extended family who I am connected to by marriage or biology and included in that are steps and halfs and partners. Some are in my day-to-day life and some I see rarely but they are all important. I also have family friends and friends who feel like chosen family who I love like they were blood. It really is far more complex than any neat package and it's all the better for it!

For Hollie de Cruz (@theyesmummum), her family set-up involves her and her partner Simon and their three boys. They each have a ten-year-old son from previous marriages, and then they have another son together.

'Families are units of love – and they can present in very different ways. Sometimes they can reduce, expand or change shape, but this doesn't alter their identity as a family. One family can't be compared to another because we are all unique. There isn't a right or wrong way for families to look, and we should be accepting of how brilliantly one-of-a-kind each unit of love is. People don't have to be with you all the time to love you all the time.'

'Don't get hung up on who you're related to and what roles they're expected to perform in your life,' says Robyn (@around_robyn), who has spoken publicly about being estranged from her mum. 'There's a massive value in people who make you feel loved, valued and safe; it doesn't matter if you share DNA.' She describes her family in the following way: 'My little brother and I were raised by my Pops in a pretty happy single-parent household and I was mummed by my brilliant Nan alongside aunties, teachers, family friends – anyone who recognised I needed a little motherly influence. I went on to replicate that dynamic by marrying the most maternal man I ever met. When I was a kid I wish I had known that I'd create the family I'd always dreamed of but it would be made up of a gaggle of similarly damaged misfits. It's a great crew to be part of. Constant cups of tea and cuddles.'

Then I threw the question of 'what is a family?' out far and wide. These are some of the answers that I heard most commonly. Take your pick of any that resonate with you:

- Marge Simpson was right when she said there is no such thing as a 'nice, normal family'. 'Normal' doesn't exist.

- Being connected by blood is irrelevant; the connection is through love.

- Family is who you choose to draw in. You are not obliged to love someone just because you are related.

- Sometimes families can take a while to figure out.

- Family is a place where you can be yourself: safe, secure and warm. It can look many different ways, but it is how it feels that is important.

- Family is just a collection of people you love most, no other labels needed. It's the place where you feel you belong.

(For more insight about talking to kids about divorce and shifts in family arrangements, head to page 114.)

Someone also introduced me to the Māori concept of *whānau*: in Māori society a family is not the nuclear family defined by Western society. It's the collective of people connected through a common ancestor, or people who are not related but who are bound together by a shared purpose. As part of that, members of the *whānau* support and empower one another. A physically and mentally healthy *whānau* is there to help the *whānau* to succeed and overcome issues. There is no feeling of isolation within a *whānau*. I love this!

Another insight that stuck with me is from the book *Happy, Healthy Minds* by The School of Life.[16] They explain that your own family might feel weird and different. But that is because you know your family best, so you get to know all the odd, crazy and personal parts.

Tom @unlikelydad and his partner Danny adopted their son Kai when he was fourteen months young and simply can't remember a time before him. Tom says: 'What might look and feel normal to you isn't the same for every child, and that's okay. It's what makes us all unique.'

It would be boring if everyone's family was the same. (I also adore the person who said, 'A pizza is still a pizza even if it has different toppings!') Families are complicated and wonderful, aren't they? But also they are the people who bring out the best and very worst in us. So it's also worth reminding your child that sometimes families that look perfect on the outside aren't always so perfect when viewed from within. Remember that nobody knows what is going on behind closed doors.

On which note, did you know that turtles aren't 'inside' their shells; they actually ARE their shells? It's not a body and an extra bit, it's all the same thing. Google it, it's absolutely mind-blowing. It also proves that what we think we see on the outside isn't necessarily what is actually on the inside.

BUT WHY DO PEOPLE GET MARRIED?

- Knee-jerk answer: haven't a clue.

- Cynic's answer: they get caught up with the party and the dress.

- Realist answer: financial security.

- Romantic answer: love.

Of course, the truth is all and none of these things. My kids ask questions about marriage a lot. We have been to a couple of family weddings recently and they were very caught up in the idea of the party and getting to wear smart outfits. As such, they are also livid not to have been on the guest list for our wedding day. Which was absolutely nothing personal, and totally down to the fact they weren't alive yet. So apart from the dress and the party and the cake and all that stuff, which we will dig into shortly, why on earth *do* people get hitched?

Kate Everall of @lesbemums is very clear on how she and her wife came to tie the knot. Why do people get married? 'To celebrate their love with their nearest and dearest, or because that country's law dictates it. It's a sad fact, but my wife wouldn't have been named as the "other parent" on our son's birth certificate if he had been conceived "out of wedlock". If we had conceived him in a clinic, then that would have been a different story, but because that wasn't a viable option, we had to be married/civil partnered before conception.'

Kate went on to say that, of course, marriage and the motivations to do it are hugely personal, pointing out that she knows couples who have been together for decades and haven't seen the value in marriage, as they know within themselves that they love each other and that's all that matters.

Holly June Smith, a celebrant and life coach, reminded me to think of the history of it. The practice of marriage was established to address the societal pressure of women *needing* a husband. Women were 'married off'. And marriage was a means for women to access financial rights. Similarly, there was a stigma around having a baby out of wedlock, or indeed even living together.

So why are we still doing it? WHY are people getting married?

For the 500 people I asked, their reasons for marriage were varied. *Commitment. Pregnancy. Blindly following societal expectation. Security. Stability. Visa. Religion.* 'Because he asked me' was a fairly common response. As was the notion of tradition. *'It felt like the next step . . . I wanted the same surname as my children.'*

There were many more romantic answers, too. *'To show the world we were in it forever . . . To publicly demonstrate our commitment to one another . . . Because he was so much more than a boyfriend . . . Because I wanted to be her wife.'*

Holly June Smith confirms that these answers match her experiences as a celebrant. The main motivator is a couple wanting to celebrate their love for each other, to cement a relationship and to fuse two backgrounds together.

What else? When talking to kids about marriage, it's also important to split the idea of marriage from a wedding. Especially when a) we continue to be peddled a fairy-tale wedding-day ideal, and b) kids love a party. But kids need to understand that marriage is about much more than the big day itself.

And I am all for a party to celebrate love. But not if it lands you on the back foot before you've begun – with debt and family arguments or, in my case, in a terrible patch of anxiety.

That said, I have changed my mind a little about weddings recently. Covid-19, like any major life event, has made me realise that there is beauty in celebrating these milestones. Life can change in a minute and then what?

If my kids were looking to get hitched I'd say: go for it! But make it the day you want, not the one you feel you ought to have, and don't let the party become more important than the commitment you are making.

I also wanted to sneak in this additional 'I wish I had known that . . .' here from Kate Everall:

> **When I was a kid, I wish I had known that . . .**
> I could take my time when it came to making decisions and that changing your mind is a viable option. Too often, our children are rushed into what job they want to do when they grow up, who they want to marry, what house they want to buy, when really they should just be living and concentrating on being happy (or at least content)! Life is too short and all that.
>
> Kate Everall @lesbemums

Some talking points:

- You don't have to get married.

- Boys can marry boys and girls can marry girls.

- A marriage is not just about a wedding.

- Marriage can come in different forms, such as civil partnership. It is also different in other countries and religions.

- No. You can't marry your sister. You don't need to. You have her to love anyway.

- Marrying someone is one of the biggest decisions you'll make. But when it's right it should feel the easiest.

- It's okay to stop being married if it doesn't make you happy.

- Finding someone who loves you is brilliant but they don't have to be your partner: your friends love you too and it's also important to love yourself.

- If it is your child asking you about marriage, remember what the personal implications are for them in your answer.

Why *not* get married?

Speaking to barrister Sarah Langford was an eye-opener. Statistically, half of marriages end in divorce and at the time of writing the average wedding costs £30,355. Ordinarily, you'd never bet such a huge sum of money on something with such terrible odds. When I asked, these were the reasons people gave me for choosing not to say 'I do': *'Money money money*

. . . Couldn't justify it . . . Always something else to buy . . . It's not 1920! . . . To rebel against societal expectations . . . He never asked . . . Not important to us . . . Seen it be the end of many relationships . . . Can't stand the wasted money or the hype . . . Marriage doesn't mean anything to me.'

All of these objections are valid. And in light of them, not in spite of them, what conclusions can we draw? The main one is that marriage is not a must. People get married for all sorts of reasons. The most important one being love. But that doesn't mean they love each other more than another couple who are not married.

And while we're about it, being in a relationship is optional too. It's not something you have to strive for.

The concept of being with someone forever, with or without the ring, is an extraordinary thing. Logic tells you it is a weird concept. But then you meet someone and you think, 'I would like to have you by my side from this day forward.'

Ben and I celebrated ten years married last year and it has been both harder and easier than expected. Here I looked to journalists Anna Whitehouse and Matt Farquharson, who in their book *Where's My Happy Ending?*[17] explore how we navigate the part from 'I do' to 'death do us part'. The pair (themselves a husband and wife) interviewed tons of people from all walks of life and asked them their opinion about the key to marital happiness. There is a huge amount of insight in the book, but what stuck with me was the couple's own reflections off the back of it.

Anna told me that on reflection she now sees that you don't become married to someone on your wedding day. The marrying part happens in the bits life throws at you or, as she puts it, 'through miscarriage, redundancy, postnatal depression, all the dark idiosyncrasies that lurk between two people'. Woooahh, there is so much truth in that; it's one thing saying the vows, it's another living them. You might envisage the 'for better' part, but how do you manage when faced with 'for worse'?

This is something Matt picked up on. He stressed that the idea of 'happily ever after' is a myth. He believes that collectively we have swallowed the lie that life should be a permanent fairy-tale and anything that falls short of that is shameful, or that we ourselves have failed. But that fairy-tale place doesn't really exist. Instead, he says, 'There is a place called "good enough", which is absolutely something to be proud of.'

It definitely isn't like the movies, but to have someone choose to stick by your side for better or worse (e.g. when you are in your fleece dressing gown or yelling at them to go buy you some stool-softener NOW whilst trying to get that post-baby poo out) is humbling. Incidentally, of the 500 people I asked, about 86 per cent would do it again. Which sounds like good numbers to me.

One last thought. Author Glennon Doyle, talking to Brené Brown, asks us to ask ourselves if we would want our own marriage for our kids? I'll leave that powerful question for you to ponder.

BUT WHY DO PEOPLE GET DIVORCED?

Though this is a complex and potentially emotional subject, it's probably good to start with some facts. Divorce means that two people are separating because they no longer want to be married.

There is a great site called divorcedgirlsmiling.com that is a treasure trove of advice. One line that jumped out at me was: 'Come up with your elevator pitch.' That might sound odd, but there's such logic in it. Find a way of describing a new relationship status, for those who ask, that doesn't involve raking through any complicated details – that could not only be tough for you, but is also best avoided when kids might be within earshot.

Beyond that there are themes that came up over and over again when I researched this:

- Don't air dirty laundry in public. That includes social media. Nothing good ever came of it.

- Allow yourself time. A few people suggested that two years is a realistic timeframe for truly coming out the other side. Sounds like a long time? It's only a parameter and hopefully one that will be followed by decades of happiness. Don't know about you, but I'd prefer someone was frank about these things (unlike whichever prat suggested that having a baby gets magically easier from the twelve-week mark – what lies!).

Now the next point is a big one and might sound counter-intuitive, but prioritise finding a way to have as positive a relationship with your ex as possible.

'Try not to hate each other,' says Amy Ransom, who has just released her fourth book, *The Soul-Soaring Virtues of Separation*.[18] 'Try to focus on the amazing kids you had together. You liked each other once; it didn't work out, that's all. Sharing your kids is hard, it goes against your instincts and never quite feels right (even though you're desperate for a break). Remember the bigger picture of the value of your kids having the best relationship possible with both parents.'

Kiera O'Mara, who wrote about Life After Divorce for Mother of All Lists[19], adds that even if you don't feel like being amicable, try to be the bigger person. 'I understand that this is not always possible but if it is possible, it is such a good thing, for everyone involved. However bad it is between you and your ex, your kids do not need to know that. They can be spared the details. They have two parents and, assuming you both love them, then they don't need to be in the middle of an argument or used against one another. It is the children who will suffer.'

Avoid comparing your situation to others'. It's useful to draw from other people's experience of divorce, but no two are the same and, it goes without saying, there is no 'correct way'.

This is another point Amy is passionate about. Not comparing extends to making your own rules on how you view separation: 'It doesn't have to be miserable,' she says. 'It doesn't have to be bleak. I realise not everyone separates amicably. That it is not always mutual. That said, I think there comes a time where you can choose how you want it to frame your life. I decided early on that separation was going to make everything better for all of us. It had to. Otherwise, why was I not ploughing on with my marriage? Mostly, this is how we live. I refuse to maroon myself in a place society might like to stick me. Where separation is a disaster. A sad statistic. A failure. Don't get me wrong. There are days when

I have felt like a failure but these are few and far between now. There have also been times when I have felt uncomfortable not being part of a parenting couple. But we make our own rules. Because I want our separation to be inclusive, as far as it can be. I want my kids to have as much love as possible, from wherever it comes. It is *so* exhausting living amidst sadness and resentment. And whilst there may be days like that, I want those to be the exception, not the rule. So we will *always* make our own rules.'

There really is no sugar-coating divorce for your kids. However, believe it or not, it is possible to find more positives than you might expect. Hollie de Cruz wrote a surprisingly uplifting piece for Mother of All Lists called Surviving Divorce.[20] Here's an extract from it:

- I had two big fears about my marriage ending.

- The first was how it would affect our then five-year-old son. My parents separated when I was nineteen and it completely winded me emotionally. How would a five-year-old deal with that weight of pain and confusion?

- It turns out, pretty bloody amazingly.

- You realise that what counts is their experience of you together, and transparency. Kids are smart. They know when they're being duped and they don't like it. Trust is everything.

- My second fear was the shame. The shame of failing.

- Shame is a big emotion, but it's all about other people. It's a feeling that serves your own wellbeing in no way at all.

- I was afraid that people would feel sorry for me.

- There's no way to really know if those fears are legitimate until it happens. So you've got to just face the fear head on.

- I very quickly realised that no one pitied me. They just wanted the best for me. Because they're awesome.

- Telling your child is worse in your head than it is in reality. In my experience.

- Make sure you're being age-appropriate. You need to give them enough information without overwhelming them.

- The most important thing for them to hear is that you both love them.

- Let your child know they can talk to you about what's happening. Anytime. I think they internalise less if they know there's a safe and welcome place to talk about things.

- Make sure you have people to do that with too. Talking is GOOD.

- It gets easier. Fears ease, emotions settle, routines become calmer and clearer.

- And you are way more resilient than you realise. You WILL be okay.

- You will learn more about yourself on your own than you ever will with someone else. That's an amazing opportunity to be embraced.

- The better you know yourself, the happier you'll be further down the line, with or without someone else. And ultimately you realise you don't need anybody else. Really. If and when you want a new relationship, you'll be wanting it rather than needing it.

- Amongst all the fear/anger/sadness/confusion, I finally recognised that this was an opportunity. This was life pushing me in another direction. This was a chance to come home to myself.

- Every experience holds within it a blessing of some kind. Trust the process.

Ahhh, she is so wise. Talking to all sorts of people about this, I wanted to acknowledge that divorce feels like a scary word and certainly not one we hope becomes part of the narrative of our kids' childhood, but again and again parents tell me they wished they had known that we are stronger than we think! More resilient than we realise. It WILL be okay. With work and communication, starting with answering questions mindfully, separation needn't be negative.

BUT WHY IS IT SOME GIRLS
LOVE GIRLS?

Short answer: anyone can love anyone. Love is love, that is part of the beauty of it.

Or as Jules Von Hep, founder of the Isle of Paradise skincare brand, put it: 'A human being is a human being, and love is love. You might love a boy at one time, then a girl the other – see how you feel around the person as an individual. Let your heart rule who you love, not your head.'

Longer answer? This is the moment to consider opening up the conversation around sexuality. Sexual orientation simply means who you are attracted to.

There is a meme that goes round Instagram that says, 'People nowadays say that LGBTQ education isn't appropriate for young children but will ask a little girl as early as Reception whether she has a boyfriend.' That stuck with me.

I was inspired by the pointers on Young Stonewall's site (youngstonewall.org.uk):

- It isn't possible to tell someone's sexual orientation from their appearance.

- The only way to actually know someone's sexual orientation is by hearing it from them.

- Figuring out sexual orientation happens at different times for different people. Some people know when they are young, while others work it out when they're much older. Lots would say they are continually exploring what floats their boat.

- Nobody has to pick a label to describe who they love or are attracted to.

- No one knows what causes a person's sexual orientation (or if there is a specific reason, as Stonewall says, 'science hasn't cracked it yet').

- But one thing is for sure: who you're attracted to isn't a choice. It's something that 'just happens', and makes each of us who we are.

And here are some explainers of different terms:

- Lesbian – girls who fancy girls (bear in mind some girls may prefer to be called 'gay', while others prefer 'lesbian').

- Gay – when boys fancy boys or girls fancy girls. Though 'gay' most frequently refers to boys, it's not always the case and can apply to girls too.

- Bisexual/bi – this is when people fancy a range of people. This could mean a boy fancying other boys and girls, as well as people who are non-binary.

- Straight/heterosexual – when boys fancy girls and vice versa.

LGBTQ+ is an umbrella term which embraces a plethora of sexual orientations and preferences of the 'not-exclusively-heterosexual-and-monogamous' majority.

There are more labels including queer, pansexual, asexual, transgender and intersex. I've gone into the last two a little more on page 77–8.

Some people will feel that these words describe their feelings, while others won't. Your sexual orientation is personal and it's your business whether or not you decide to use a label.

Of course, many people don't like labels; however, in some instances it is handy to have common words everyone understands. For example, say Stonewall, 'a sexual health clinic might hold a "lesbian drop-in" session to offer help just to women who fancy women. The fact that everybody knows what is meant by a service for lesbians means that the right people will use it, which is really important.'

So what else is there to consider teaching kids about sexuality?

First of all, it is fluid! Some people may only like boys or girls. Some might change. And nothing is ever set in stone. (Though as a side note, one respondent told me, 'Assume I am bi forever, unless I say otherwise. Having a boyfriend doesn't suddenly make me straight.')

Another person said: 'When I came out, I felt pressured to pick a convenient label of "gay", even though I have since learned that "bi" fits me better.'

Again it's great to get away from the idea of 'normal'. As someone messaged me to say, they wished they had known when they were younger that it is 'not strange or abnormal for same-sex people to love each other'.

This is not something for kids' ears, but I also had a few people message to say they were straight but they got turned on by girl-on-girl porn. My answer to that would be simply that it is what it is!

However, there is value in being realistic about how unfortunately you may still come across people who aren't as open-minded as they could be. Kate Everall gave this advice: 'Be honest, depending on the age: explain that not everyone will always agree with who they love, but as long as they're happy, then that's all that matters. It may be worth educating yourself to prepare for certain conversations, especially if you don't have any LGBTQ+ friends or family members to ask. This is potentially going to be a grey area for you too! Stonewall and The Proud Trust are great resources for information and advice.'

Or perhaps Jules' response is a better fit for you: 'Being attracted to the same sex is completely fine, it's the way you were born and is not a choice – this is who you are. Those who judge others on their sexuality merely show they don't understand the subject – and any negative behaviour around sexuality is merely an expression of inner confusion.'

So is there anything you should AVOID telling kids about sexuality? In short, no. Keep the lines of communication age-appropriate but open.

Whatever your sexual orientation, navigating the world of being attracted to other humans is wonderful but confusing. Much like the idea of 'best friends' at school, there were people who appeared to find this part of growing up easy; my bet is it didn't feel as easy on the inside as it may have looked on the outside.

You can never, in my experience, choose who you fall in love with. It is wonderful, complex and occasionally inconvenient, but when it happens it's totally unavoidable.

From a parenting point of view, you should be there to help your child navigate the subject and to answer questions, but also be conscious of striking a balance by not forcing them to open up to you. Instead let your child know that if they want to talk, they can do so.

What to say if your child comes out to you:

I received much insightful advice around the notion of kids coming out. Some people don't identify with coming out, instead believing they should just focus on living their authentic selves. And of course it's worth pointing out that heterosexuals don't 'come out' so why do we expect it for those with other sexual orientations?

Many described the experience of opening up to family as utterly terrifying but liberating: being aware of potential fear and judgement while feeling exhilarated to be free.

Others talked of feeling as if they had to come out on a daily basis. It's not 'one and done'. In some ways you have to do it to everyone you ever meet. Lizzie Hope-Dyer, who got married in June 2019, said: 'I've been with my wife for five years and bumped into an old (conservative Christian) friend last weekend. Introducing my wife to him felt like coming out all over again. I could talk for hours on this topic – with my Christian background it's been a tough ride and I've lost a couple of friends in the process . . . but my wife is soooooo worth it all!' Ahhhh, love that last line.

Truthfully, the moment is as much about those who are on the receiving end of the news as it is on the person doing the coming out. While most parents might hope to be accepting, they may still be shocked and surprised, even if they expected it. Give yourself time to adjust.

Listen, listen, listen. Make space for your kids to talk as much or as little as they want. Be supportive but non-invasive. Don't try to fix them or ask if it's a phase.

This heartfelt email I received touches on some of the complexity of the issue:

Hi Clemmie, saw your post about the LGBTQIA+ community and wanted to write to you in a bit of a longer format. I grew up straight, had heterosexual relationships, fancied boys and imagined marrying a man. Then when I was twenty-five I realised I was in love with a girl, which was confusing and scary. I was panicking about my sexuality; I knew I still fancied boys and hadn't really ever been attracted to women before, but I realised I didn't need to work out what label I now fell under. I wanted to be with Sophie, my now girlfriend, and that was it.

So I never had a big coming out. I didn't tell people I was gay, I just told them I had a girlfriend. And in this world that is becoming ever more accepting, none of my friends had any response other than, 'Fantastic!'

But my parents didn't. They were confused, thought I had been hiding that I was a lesbian. Living in denial and lying to them about my sexuality. And it took a long time to convince them otherwise. I still don't even know if I have.

So my advice to all parents is simply to accept what their child is saying. Trust them, believe them and support it. Even if it doesn't make sense. My parents kept saying they didn't understand. And at that point I didn't really understand either. So while I was navigating all the changes in my sexuality, I was also dealing with the breakdown of my relationship with my parents and feeling that I had to have answers to everyone's questions.

There is so much content available now about coming out and the LGBTQ+ community, but I just wish there was more of a space for those of us who just fall in love. We don't need labels to explain it, we don't

need it to be justified to know it's real. I wish that
my children don't need to feel they have to 'come out'.
I want them to know that to love someone is special
and pure no matter what the person's gender is. And
that they will be accepted in that no matter what.

It's okay to have a reaction but don't make it a big deal. Most of all, remind your children you love them unconditionally. That you want them to be happy.

'Keep focused on your child. Keep your feelings out of it.' This advice is particularly pertinent here, but it is valuable across the board. For me, that is exactly the role of a parent. We show that we have feelings but to be an adult means we should never be burdening our kids with them.

Be honest with yourself and be curious about whether any underlying emotion you might feel is about the person in question or because of fear and judgement or shifted expectations. After all, these days being queer doesn't rule out grandkids!

It's okay to feel you need support yourself if your child comes out. Head online: there is tons of information out there. And remember, as one respondent said, 'The person who is coming out and exploring their sexuality has a lot to deal with without being everyone's teacher along the way.'

Check in with siblings too. Give advice to relatives on how to be inclusive and more neutral. And, of course, give 'em a cuddle! More of these, please. Wow, this last year has been dry on the old hug front, hasn't it?

In conclusion, the details of sexuality are irrelevant; what is important are healthy relationships (that applies to the sexual part too). More on that in the 'But why do we have "love"?' section later.

When I was a kid, I wish I had known . . . what was ahead for me. I grew up thinking the person I am was wrong. I convinced myself I'd find a girlfriend, get married and have a baby. I remember thinking, 'It won't be fun, but I just have to . . .' But I'd love to show that young boy the picture he has now; the life he has made with boys . . . I wish I had known that would be possible back then.

Tom Cox @unlikelydad

JOINING BIT THREE:

JUDGE YOURSELF, NOT OTHERS

> *The world is messy. There are ambiguities.*
> *People who do really good stuff have flaws.*
> Barack Obama

Setting ourselves 'all or nothing' ideals is unrealistic. Expecting humans to be anything other than humans is the road to nowhere. Sitting in a place of judgement stifles the opportunity for change, particularly in yourself.

In the early weeks of the Covid-19 pandemic, I would take my 'once a day' walk. Like everyone, I savoured that experience and I had a new appreciation for the smaller things (my camera roll is full of pictures of flowers), but as well as that, something less life-affirming was afoot. I would walk round Peckham Rye and absent-mindedly judge everyone: were they abiding by the rules? Should they have been out? Was it really their household they were with? And was that truly 2 metres?

After a few weeks of doing this (it felt like a lifetime, such was the warped nature of that time) and habitually judging everyone, I realised that I was making a great success of ruining my own experience. The upshot was I was returning home sixty minutes later with a mind full of unanswered questions and negative emotions that left me feeling worse than if I had stayed indoors.

And the root of that was judgement.

Another example of misguided and frankly pointless judgement is a parenting one. A mum I knew who worked full time but always picked her kid up from school on a Friday told me that although she loved that moment with her child, she felt judged by the other mums who were clearly regulars at the school gates.

Though I could absolutely empathise with that feeling, I asked her to consider it from the other perspective. Perhaps those other mums weren't judging; maybe they were looking at her in admiration or envy. Maybe they were worried that *they* were being judged – that as a working mum she was judging the stay-at-homes for having nowhere else to be but at the school gates?

How does all this apply to answering questions from our kids? Try to approach each situation without judgement. Come to any situation as neutrally as you can. Take things based on how you see them. If you have preconceived ideas, be prepared to shift them.

In reference to call-out culture and cancel culture, what is there to say about it other than it is toxic? It comes down to a belief that other people shouldn't have an opinion that differs from our own. But who wants to live in a world with single perspectives?

Call-out culture doesn't allow for diversity of thought, for exploration. It certainly doesn't allow for growth. Of course we should be mindful of what we put out in the world. But a post I wrote five years ago, based on what I knew then, based on the day I was having then, based on the person I was then, shouldn't define me forever.

Anyone who has been at the receiving end of any kind of trolling will relate to how disconnected it feels to be judged by someone who doesn't know you. Having any kind of digital presence (which, let's face it, the majority of us do now) means you are inevitably opening yourself up to criticism, but the issue is that it feels one-sided. Someone is judging you for XYZ, but not taking the time to reflect on their own behaviour.

We have to get used to differing ideas and not default to being defensive, unless of course someone is being deliberately offensive. Calling out for the sake of calling out gets in the way of useful conversation, useful feedback and positive criticism.

Stop judging, start listening. And though it would be easy to default and say STOP JUDGING ME, remember that is out of your control. All you can do is stop judging others. Check yourself and if you haven't got anything useful to say, don't say it. If you don't agree with someone's view, a better response might be: 'That's interesting. I don't agree but that's okay.'

If Mother of All Lists and my podcasts *Honestly* and *But Why?* and now researching this has taught me anything, it is that everyone has a story. They might be in the midst of something tough, or grew up in challenging circumstances, or maybe they are just coming up for air from a bad patch.

That isn't to say 'life stuff' should give us an automatic right to do what we like. But it does mean that we should treat everyone with kindness and assume that they are doing their best until proved otherwise.

And when you do find yourself being judgemental, check in with where you are at with yourself. Is it coming from your own stress or insecurity? (The mum at the school gates.) Is it because you are feeling compromised? (Me in Peckham Rye, struggling with the pandemic.) Is my default to judgement actually a sign that I need to show myself a bit of kindness? Rather than anyone else being 'wrong', perhaps I am in need of help to feel 'right'?

I am no expert; these are just tricks I use to try and help myself. I want my kids to be curious about other people. I want them to be interested in their whole stories, rather than making a snap judgement based on a page of it. The American Tibetan Buddhist Pema Chödrön advises us to recognise our shared humanity, because that, she says, is when 'compassion becomes real'.

As the Roman emperor and Stoic philosopher Marcus Aurelius said: 'Waste no more time arguing about what a good man should be. Be one.'

When I was a kid, I wish I had known that . . . my parents didn't know everything. I think when we're kids we hold our parents up in this impenetrable high esteem. We naturally see them as our beacons of truth and wisdom, and as a child I think it can give us quite a one-dimensional perspective of our parents' full experience. We trust them to be all-knowing and completely trustworthy, but I wish I'd had more exposure to their flaws and human nature. I think if I'd seen them struggle more I would have been better equipped with self-compassion in my own struggles, rather than having to unpick these subconscious beliefs that my confidence and emotions should be steadfast. I guess I wish I'd known that people get it wrong and have bad days, and that's okay. We're not meant to be succeeding, we're meant to be learning.

Hollie de Cruz @theyesmummum

4

QUESTIONS ABOUT
COMPLEX FEELINGS

I am an emotionally complex Pisces. (Yes, I am into astrology. And before anyone mentions the fact that the astrology chart got rejigged in 2020 and I am now an Aquarius, I am just not having it. 2020 brought about some serious changes in the world and I am not prepared to let being stripped of my Piscean identity be yet another.)

ANYWAY. I am just emotional. For as long as I can remember I was made to believe that being sensitive or indeed 'over-sensitive' was a bad thing – but the older I get, the more comfortable I am with it. I don't know what feelings are like for other people – maybe mine are closer to the surface than other people's? Maybe other people just don't talk about them as much?

The way I look at it is that I see my feelings in hypercolour. They are full-on (and occasionally overwhelming). But for me that's preferable to existing with muted emotions.

Also, feelings are there whether we choose to acknowledge them or not. I'm not suggesting we need to put them front and centre all the time. But they are the bit that make us human, and are fundamental for true connection.

Quick bit of housekeeping: in this section you'll see the questions blend together more than they do in other chapters, the reason being that feelings don't sit in isolation from one another. Not only are they linked, but the ways we should think and talk to our kids about them are linked too.

BUT WHY DO WE HAVE FEELINGS?

When I read this, I hear myself say 'WHHYYYYYYYYYY?' in a dramatic way. I fantasise about being super free and unemotional. Ha! But actually feelings are absolutely vital.

Feelings are there to link the physical and psychological parts of ourselves. Feelings are the feedback from your body about your physical and emotional state. They are there to let you know what's going on with you. They are your own gauge or barometer.

The School of Life's book *Happy, Healthy Minds*, which I highly recommend for exploring emotional wellbeing in kids, goes one step further and reminds us that the brain is PART of our bodies. Sounds obvious? Maybe, but weirdly it's easy to forget. And importantly, the brain sends signals on behalf of the rest of our body and they show up as feelings.

This means that sometimes wires get crossed. For example, ideally the brain would simply say you are hungry, stop trying to put together that flat-pack doll's house and eat a sandwich; instead it gives us an overwhelming sense of rage.

Such a good insight, right? Not only is it a great reminder of why feelings are so important, it's also a great trick to teach our kids when talking about feelings: if you find yourself having tricky emotions, remember that sometimes when the brain is feeling something it's a clue about something going on with the body.

Rather than getting caught up in the idea of the emotion, do a quick scan instead. Am I tired? Am I stressed? Am I thirsty or hungry? It's probably too hard a concept for children to understand properly, but 'am I overstimulated?' is probably why being on a tablet leads to blazing sibling rows.

An additional one is 'am I hormonal?' – ha! One of my friends confessed that whenever she finds her mother-in-law excruciatingly annoying it's usually a sign her period is due. Bearing in mind that puberty might be impacting your kids sooner than you think, it could well account for their tricky feelings sometimes too.

So feelings are very clever and useful. They are what make us human and they help us look after ourselves. I am all for embracing them, talking about them, generally being fascinated by them!

BUT WHY DO I FEEL THESE
BAD FEELINGS?

There is no such thing as 'bad feelings'.

All feelings are equal because they all do exactly the same job: they tell us what is going on with ourselves. Though we have come to associate some emotions as being bad because of the moments and experiences we attach to them, the reality is that feelings themselves are equal and equally important. Being sad or angry or worried is as important as being happy or excited.

For help with this I turned to Anna Mathur, a psychotherapist, mum of three and author of *Sunday Times* bestseller *Mind over Mother*.[21] Anna has a real talent for making sense of things in a way that marries professional insight with personal experience, and as such I am grateful for her input through this chapter, starting with her own thoughts on difficult feelings.

'The thing is,' says Anna, 'feelings might be unpleasant, they might be conflicting or make little sense, but they are valid. They are there, and the most effective way of dealing with feelings is to acknowledge them, let them be, and let them subside. We so often try to analyse, fix, change, shift or explain away feelings.'

Anna compares them to labour. Cast your mind back there, for a moment. She explains that feelings are like contractions (although thankfully emotions don't make me moo like labour does!). Each contraction has a purpose; each one gone is another one never to be experienced again; each passes.

For me that also resonated in that when you're in labour, if you try to resist or become fearful of the contractions, your adrenalin rises and they feel more painful. Instead, what you should aim to do is note them, says Anna, even voice them if you want to, and then check in with yourself later on to see if they're still there. 'Often the feeling has softened, shifted, subsided alone without you "doing" anything besides letting it do its thing.'

And how does this relate to the way we talk to our kids about negative feelings? For Anna, 'the less fearful we are of our emotions, and the more able we are to sit with them and trust them, the more able we become to guide our children through this process too.'

✳ Some homework: ✳

To explain this further, I would 'prescribe' something that helped me understand this subject: watch the Pixar movie *Inside Out*.

Even better (pro parenting tip): call it 'Movie Night' and blag getting the kids in the bath and into PJs early doors, chuck in some popcorn and suddenly a lazy Saturday afternoon is something exciting. Better still, you can pat yourself on the back because this one is educational too.

Inside Out is all about navigating feelings and demonstrates their purpose and their importance. The film's main characters are the emotions in a little girl's brain, and the storyline focuses on how to recover joy after a traumatic experience. Spoiler alert (can't believe I just wrote that, soz): brilliantly and perhaps surprisingly, Sadness rather than Joy emerges as the hero.

How? *Inside Out* shows that demonstrating seemingly less desirable (and often therefore avoided) feelings like sadness, fear and anger can have hugely important and even positive outcomes. They help us connect with other people, spot danger and indeed even heal from hard experiences.

What can we as parents learn from this? Earlier I mentioned not suppressing your own hard feelings – well, that also extends to stopping trying to prevent sadness in our kids. Or, something else we often default to, trying to CHANGE our children's feelings. Of course we should comfort them but that is different from the urge to change their legitimate emotions.

Anna explains that it's tempting to 'want to fix, to relieve, to take away. There is actually a biological release and shift that comes when tears are shed – tears are productive! They are to be shed, not halted and held in.

'Try to coach yourself through the anxiety you experience when your child is feeling something you've been taught is undesirable,' Anna continues. 'Let that wave of anxiety pass as you focus on being present. You are the anchor in their little storm, and when the thunder has rolled by, they will return to themselves. By validating them instead of moving to fix them, you are teaching them that emotions are nothing to be afraid of, and that they can come to you regardless of how they feel. When we utter, "Don't cry. Don't be silly. It will be fine. Cheer up", we are unintentionally giving them the message that they are most acceptable to us in their happy state.'

Makes sense! I don't know about you, but when I am angry or sad or stressed or confused, that is exactly when I need love and care. Of course we wish we could magically be happy, but that's not how it works!

So what else is there to consider when talking to kids about feelings? From the research I've done, these are common learnings:

Acknowledge feelings. This can be done in a few ways. The simplest way is to actually label and talk about emotions, including your own: *sorry you feel sad, I am glad you're so excited, I was angry when I dropped that glass.* Why? Give your children the language so that when they feel something, they are increasingly able to communicate it and trust that it will be heard and validated – as opposed to them acting out on it, which might lead to them being reprimanded and having the initial feeling overlooked altogether.

Sometimes if those feelings are trickier for your children to express, there are other tools to help externalise them. Playing a game or doing some art or putting on some music all spring to mind. (Any excuse for a cheeky bit of Taylor Swift – sorry not sorry!)

Separate the feeling from the action or behaviour. Rather than just 'stop kicking the trolley!', try: 'I can see you are angry that I won't buy you the magazine. But can you stop kicking the trolley?' We can't help how we feel. The key is learning to behave in an appropriate way when confronted with those feelings. It's okay to say that you wish you had a magazine; it is not okay to start kicking things in the supermarket.

'Consider the boundaries you hold around emotion for them,' says Anna. 'For example, anger is fine, but biting is not. Therefore, you listen to the anger, and you hold the boundary around the biting. Often we address the bite rather than hear the anger, and both need attention. I might say to my son, "I totally get that you're angry, I can see that you feel cross that you didn't get a turn on the slide, but it's not okay to hit." Explore other ways to exhibit these emotions, and talk about them/act them out when they aren't live or activated. For example, on a relaxed weekend morning, I might get everyone stamping around the kitchen saying, "When we're angry we can STAMP OUR FEET."' Again, this is a physical way to both externalise and in turn acknowledge a feeling.

Be aware of your reactions first. In any given situation, try to get a hold of your emotions before dealing with theirs. It's the whole 'applying your own oxygen mask' before putting it on your kid. Adding your own emotions on top of others' leads to a spiralling situation. Psychotherapist Philippa Perry talks of being a 'container' for your child's feelings, so rather than absorbing them or being part of them, you are able to 'hold' them as something separate.

Sometimes, for me, that involves actually stepping out of the room and coming back calmly and objectively. If we aren't there to change our children's feelings, we can help them navigate them in a way that feels safe and 'acceptable', says Perry.

Anna phrases it like this: 'My job is to be their anchor. That is my one, biggest and most challenging job. I can only be their anchor if I am anchored. I can only be their calm because I am calm. I can only be consistent, if I provide myself with some consistency of input. I cannot give what I myself do not have, therefore I must prioritise my own mental health and feelings much more than I do. And it requires me to look after myself, ensure my basic needs are met; ensure I'm not burnt out, resentful, impatient.' I would also add hungry to that list – that might sound niche, but it's helped me.

Eat dinner early: not only is it supposed to be good for metabolism, but I have found doing kids' bedtime with a full stomach a massive win. Not only is my patience so much better than if I am hungry, it means I can focus on them. As I tuck them in, it's often the time when they want a big chat or to ask The Important Question and that is really hard to do with a rumbling stomach.

Best case, they go to bed easily (if nobody is teething or has a cold or an itchy label or there's not a full moon) and you've got the whole night to devote to Netflix! Ha!

BUT WHY DON'T I KNOW WHAT
I AM FEELING?

Actually not knowing what you are feeling is a pretty common state of affairs.

The reason for this could be one of a few things: 1) not having the language; 2) having an amalgamation of feelings; 3) not being sure of the root of the feeling; and 4) being conflicted about your emotions.

The first point is pretty self-explanatory. Either you do not have the words to articulate what you're feeling (this is especially probable if you're a kid) or there aren't actually the words for it in the English language.

Quick aside: the German language seems to be great at producing words for subtle emotions. Take, for example, *Weltschmerz*, which means the feeling of having the weight of the world on your shoulders; *Sehnsucht* is an obsessive yearning; while *Geborgenheit* is the magical feeling that comes with security, comfort and warmth.

Ah! I love these so much. But when we don't have these nuanced words to hand it can be hard to put our finger on what's going on emotionally.

A second challenge to someone knowing what they are feeling might be that they are experiencing either two emotions at once or a mix of emotions. In our house we talk a lot about being 'happy-sad'. One example being the recent breakage of a plate that was very precious to me. Growing up, I longed for stuff with my name on. It's hard to imagine it now when personalised stuff is everywhere. But back then when we went on a school trip I'd scour the gift shop, hoping there would be a giant pencil or one of those money pots that hung around your neck with my name on, alongside the ones my more traditionally monikered mates Laura and Hannah could buy. There never was. So when Granny bought me a side plate with an illustration and 'CLEMENTINE' painted on it, I was over the moon. I treasured it.

But recently Greta took a shine to it and started serving imaginary cakes on it from her kitchen. It made me happy to see her playing with it. And then the inevitable happened. She dropped it mid-service (every waitress's worst nightmare) and it smashed in two. Though I don't regret giving it to her, it left me crying big heaving sobs to find it broken, especially so soon after Granny's death. Just like bereavement itself, it was a mix-up of feelings. When someone dies, you are sad to have lost the person, but happy to have had the opportunity to love them for as long as you did. The same applies with break-ups and redundancies too.

Knowing that it's possible to feel more than one thing at one time can help make it seem less bewildering for a child if they are experiencing this conflict of emotions. Spending some time talking it through with them helps rationalise it; other times simply explaining that it's a muddle of feelings is enough.

The third point to consider is whether your child doesn't know what they are feeling because the cause is unclear. It could be any number of things, but one that I wanted to draw attention to because it is frequently overlooked but quietly powerful is 'comparison'. The best example I can think of is one for us grown-ups: why is it that scrolling on social media often leaves us feeling 'a bit shit'? It's comparison. Looking at other people's (edited) lives can, without our awareness, result in a bunch of wobbly feelings: insecurity, jealousy, even anger and sadness, all of which can feel particularly confusing if you don't quite know what to attribute them to.

I've seen it in my kids too, talking about what other people got for Christmas or who did what for their birthday. The root is comparison and the outcome is a muddle of emotions that might be challenging to pick apart. If you want to learn about comparison there is one person to turn to: 'the world's first and only comparison coach', Lucy Sheridan, who wrote a brilliant piece for Mother of All Lists.[22] This is an extract:

- Comparison is a real thing and its effect on our lives is real. This is why, if you get platitudinal advice like 'just get over it', 'just stop looking', 'just do your own thing' when you are vulnerable in sharing your feelings, you need to exit the conversation as it's not a supportive space for you. You are entitled to every single feeling and emotion you have and you are not weak or ineffective if comparison feels acute for you.

- It's all a mirror – the sparkly and the not so nice. What you notice in others is a reflection of what is inside you too – we share so many characteristics.

- So, if you think someone's a bit smug, the chances are you are too and similarly, if you think someone is a good laugh then it's time to let your sense of humour shine as well.

- Your comparison is trying to reveal a hidden jewel of insight to you – a bit like that vintage favourite game show, *The Crystal Maze*.

- For example, if your comparison is triggered when you see someone off on holiday again, what does this tell you about your need to travel? In reality, someone else's air miles have zero to do with the fact you have been ignoring your own need to have a change of scene.

- When we compare ourselves to others, it's a form of self-abandonment, which is why our reactions can feel so emotional. It's easy to rationalise but not always helpful in the moment – be kind to yourself and come back to yourself by taking some big belly breaths when you feel it start to sting you.

- 'Cool' is a made-up thing.

- 'Popular' is a made-up thing.

- 'On trend' is a made-up thing.

- 'In with the in crowd' is a made-up thing.

- Numbers on social media denoting value or influence is a made-up thing.

- Comparison tricks us into thinking that success is a zero-sum game – that a win for someone else is a direct loss for us – but this isn't true. What you want is being held in trust for you but you have to go and meet it halfway to get it.

- Every time you compare yourself to someone else you miss a chance to back yourself and instead turn your back on yourself. That's part of the reason it feels like it really hurts.

For me, being aware of comparison in myself and in my kids is like having another tool in my 'emotional understanding armoury' – a reference point to check in against. Particularly the idea that the root of my comparison insecurity is likely to be something that's going on with me. Isn't it always? Ha!

We have touched on not having the language to describe emotions, amalgamated feelings being challenging, and sneaky causes like comparison that get in the way of our emotions.

The last point here is being conflicted about what you are feeling. The most significant example of that is positive risk-taking, and the idea of 'feeling the fear and doing it anyway'.

I don't know about you but I want to raise kids who are brave. Not foolish, but individuals who have the ability to assess risk and occasionally push themselves.

The older I've got, the more I feel the fear. Maybe it's the natural order of things? Once you become a parent you are naturally on high alert because your job is to spot all the potential dangers for your offspring (something that is particularly true when your kid first mounts one of those Micro Scooters!).

Try as we might, we can't continue to be the danger-spotters forever. Or as Fi and Jane say on their brilliant podcast *Fortunately*, we can't be 'curling parents' (curling as in the sport), forever there smoothing the ground around our children and hoping that they will glide through life. That just isn't realistic.

Simply put, if we always make the decision for them about whether or not they need a coat, they'll never learn when the right time for a coat is.

And the only way to teach them is to let them occasionally go out in the cold or rain without one. Of course, I am not advocating locking them out to get hypothermia, but you get my point. We need them to understand danger, but also learn the benefit of risk.

Beyond that, when I picture my most joyous moments in childhood, they often involve danger: tree swings, climbing hay bales, braving the deep end. I am sure there were some accidents along the way, but I don't remember them.

We want kids to experience all of that. And to raise adults who are independent and capable of making decisions to keep themselves safe, and don't shrink from their opportunities in an environment of safety-driven fear.

How do we start? In their book, *The Thriving Child*,[23] Dr William Stixrud and Ned Johnson talk about the notion of 'Your Call'. To be clear, this isn't handing over responsibility. Kids need boundaries and nobody wants a home run by small people. Nor is it about absolving yourself of responsibility. Instead they say, 'When it comes to a decision about your kids' lives, you should not be deciding things they are capable of deciding themselves.' We want them to learn to feel that odd sensation of apprehension and do it anyway.

How do we make danger not so dangerous for children? The psychologist Lev Vygotsky, whose work focused on how culture affects cognitive development, suggests an approach built around a framework of: 'I show you how to do something, then I step back and let you have a go with me watching.' That makes sense to me.

We have to challenge ourselves not to mollycoddle them or 'smooth the bumps'. In an article titled 'How to Raise a Happy Child – What Every Parent Needs to Know',[24] Matthew Syed cited work by Professor Grant Schofield. He worked with schools to open up a nearby area of waste ground for kids to roam free in during breaks, rather than playing in the usual 'safer' playground (with rubberised floors, etc). Do you know what they discovered? There were FEWER injuries than usual. Fascinating. And it didn't stop there: it also translated to better behaviour when the kids were in school. Which teaches us that learning to be alert to risk is preparation for self-preservation beyond the playground.

Sometimes when you experience that nervous feeling, it is easy to instinctively see it as anxiety and, for me at least, that can soon spiral.

Instead I actively remind myself to see it as excitement – I actually refer to it as 'school disco nerves' because that's my earliest memory of that sense of nervous anticipation.

Also, that adrenalin-fuelled feeling is often your body preparing to bring your A-game; it's where you 'get your wings'. This vein of thinking also reminds me of one of the posters on the wall at Facebook HQ, which read: 'What would you do if you weren't afraid?'

I adore this. Taking risks is where new business, new adventures, love and thrills come from. Who are we to deny our kids that? Doubt kills more dreams than failure ever did. Better an 'oops' than a 'what if'. Even if it does lead to a few tears.

And as for the question 'But why don't I know what I am feeling?', there isn't a neat answer, but there is a handy bit of reassurance to remember that it's okay not to know. And not only is it okay, it's also very common; feelings are complex things.

BUT WHY IS THAT PERSON SAD ALL THE TIME?

This is less about answering questions from kids and more something I felt needed to be included when navigating conversations around feelings. The fact is that experiencing difficult feelings is part of being a human.

But where is the line between feeling off and needing help?

When things feel grey or particularly difficult, I have some tried and tested 'back pocket' strategies that tend to help stabilise me: eating well, sleeping well, moving my body, getting off technology, getting into nature and trying to talk about how I am feeling. I don't drink alcohol but if I still did then I would look to reduce that and also be wary of the amount of caffeine I am consuming.

If, after two weeks of trying all the above and seeing no shift, then I would try to find the strength to reach out. As a rule of thumb: if I am even starting to ask myself 'do I need help?', then it probably means I do.

If you too are struggling, go to your doctor or reach out to a charity. You wouldn't think twice about seeking help with a physical injury. This should be just the same.

Remember, you are loved. And know this: the lights will come back on. Mental unwellness is like gaslighting yourself – it convinces you that things are doomed, that nobody cares. Neither is true. Hang in there.

I asked Alain de Botton about his understanding of emotional wellbeing and he commented on how there has been a huge shift of attitude towards mental health in recent years. 'If things didn't go well in your mind [in the past] you were written off as a lunatic,' he said.

The important shift is that we have to stop relegating mental unwellness to some freakish category and see it as something that is likely to strike all of us at some point in our lives: no more rare or shameful than it is to injure your toe or to get sunburnt. These feelings are just part of being a vulnerable person in a complex world.

✳ Things I have learned about feelings: ✳

- That not acknowledging feelings doesn't make them go away.

- In fact, by not acknowledging them we are probably denying ourselves the chance to move on from them. Speaking them out loud or having someone else do it is a great step towards being able to observe them rather than letting them define us.

- Feel the feeling, don't become it.

- Our thoughts can lie to us. I remember the first time I heard that – it blew me away.

- We have to practise sitting with uncomfortable feelings. Feeling awkward or embarrassed isn't dangerous.

- We need to stop judging our feelings (or the feelings of others) and rather observe them.

- There is strength in softness and being vulnerable is courageous (go watch Brené Brown's TED Talk, 'The Call to Courage' – it will blow your mind).

- Feelings don't always fit into neat boxes. See 'happy-sad', page 143.

- Just because someone cries a lot doesn't mean they aren't happy. Just because someone looks happy on the surface doesn't mean they aren't sad underneath.

- Feeling all the feelings makes us human.

- We have to work to stop the feelings consuming us. But the more we do that, the easier it becomes.

- Sensitivity is a good thing.

And the next question is a big one. So big, in fact, I'm giving it its own section.

BUT WHY CAN'T I JUST BE HAPPY?

Sorry, kid. That ain't how life works.

I've been guilty of 'chasing happiness'. Which sounds great, but what I am increasingly understanding is that it's like a dog chasing its tail.

Happiness is not a destination. And if it was, if we did find a utopia where the sun always shone and they served sushi and there was time to read books and swim and have long meals with family and friends, we'd find fault in it.

Don't believe me? Think of those blazing rows or massive strops you've had on holiday. Or as someone once said: sunshine all the time makes a desert.

Happiness happens when you let go of what you hoped or imagined something was going to be.

Motherhood is a great example of that. With each child, I lowered the bar of what I thought the first six months was going to be like and each time I was pleasantly surprised. Rather than chasing the idea of them sleeping through the night for the first time (what a joke), I revelled in a four-hour unbroken block.

New motherhood isn't a glorious merry-go-round of happiness – neither is life itself – but there are many moments of joy. Even tiddly ones like the smell of a newborn's head. They are the bits worth focusing on.

Two things can stand in the way of happiness, particularly if you're a new parent:

The first is guilt. Research showed me that parents felt guilty about not finding being with their kids joyful.

The other thing is being preoccupied with how a moment looks from the outside. Zoe Blaskey, founder of online self-empowerment platform Motherkind, taught me to constantly check in with 'how something feels, rather than becoming preoccupied with how it looks'. This is particularly relevant in the era of Pinterest and social media.

Joy happens on the inside. It might not look like you think. We are taught that it feels exciting and wild (much like love). But joy can be a calmer sensation, contented, mellow. Often we can't even spot it. Stop trying to manufacture it and start noticing. Try going on a walk with a kid – they have the natural ability to slow down.

And of course, even on a lovely walk with kids picking daisies or noticing insects, there will be moments where you have to persuade them to put their shoes on or carry the scooter. Don't let one take away from the other. Taking the rough with the smooth, feeling excited, bored, joyful and infuriated is what it is all about. Remember happy-sad. Living a good life isn't about being deliriously happy all the time.

Observe your feelings:

Through daily meditation I've learned that . . . Ha! I tried writing that with a straight face. I have always wanted to be the type of person who could say that. And now I can! Lockdown pushed me to dig deep into trying to steady myself among the chaos and after many failed attempts I now find ten minutes each morning to try to connect with myself.

Though I am far from finding spiritual enlightenment (I'm sure that is coming any day now), I have learned to try to observe my feelings rather than letting them absorb me. This takes me to 'I am observing some anxiety', not 'I am anxious'.

I am not my feelings. And you are not your feelings. Wild concept, hey?

In my lowest periods of mental health, I worried that the newly anxious person I had become was just who I was. The more I let it be part of me, the more it consumed me. Until just before getting diagnosed with generalised anxiety disorder, I could barely recognise myself. I had gone from fun, social, brave Clemmie to anxious Clemmie. And worse still, I was hating on that Clemmie.

But with CBT and time, I was able to step back and rationalise the uncomfortable sensation of panic as just being a moment. And one that would pass. I was not anxious Clemmie, I was just Clemmie who really didn't like it when the tube stopped at a red light.

Feelings are important gauges, but allowing them to spiral and inhabit us means they can begin to interfere with our lives: getting stuff done, making plans, enjoying the moment. So acknowledge the feelings you have. Reflect on how and why you are feeling something, then in the words of Queen Elsa: 'Let it go. Let it go . . .'

Same applies to our kids. Label what they are feeling, talk it through, resist the urge to escalate the emotion. Holding on to a negative thought or revisiting it can make it grow.

Do you get what I mean? Feelings aren't to be ignored but they aren't there to hold us hostage either.

Clinical psychologist Dr Lucy Maddox's book *Blueprint*[25] is about how our childhood shapes us and is a hugely insightful introduction to child development studies. She wrote a great piece for Mother of All Lists, which explains how strong adult feelings can be hangovers from experiences we had as children.[26] Here's an extract:

- Child development has loads to say about how we develop a sense of who we are. One of my favourite theories acknowledges that this might not get resolved by the time we reach 'adulthood'.

- James Marcia's theory of identity formation acknowledges that we can be knocked off balance by positive events as well as negative events throughout our lives. A promotion, a new relationship, a move that we have been planning for ages, can still make us feel disoriented in our sense of who we are.

- Being knocked off balance like this and then reaching some kind of equilibrium again is totally normal, the stuff of grown-up life, and so are those 3 a.m. existential panics that crop up every so often.

- Our sense of self includes a sense of self-consciousness, which although is not as painfully awkward as in our teenage years, still hangs about a bit and enables us to take a view on who we are, and maybe also who we want to be.

- By looking back at who we were, we can sometimes move forward in a slightly different direction, or at least have a better sense of where we've come from.

- That's why I think we should all know about this stuff. It can be useful, and it might help us be a little kinder to ourselves.

And to close: one last gem from Anna Mathur. She told me she has a little thing she says to her kids when she puts them to bed. She says, 'I love you when you're happy, I love you when you're sad. I love you when you're grumpy/mad/cheeky/ cross/wild.'

It's true, isn't it? I love my own kids through their feelings and am happy to sit beside them as they feel any or all of them.

JOINING BIT FOUR:

THINKING ABOUT THINKING

Normalise changing your opinion when presented with new information.

Source unknown
(made famous by illustrator Tyler Elise)

Before I started doing what I do now (whatever that is), I spent twelve years of my career in advertising agencies as a creative. It was an amazing job – I loved the work hard/play even harder vibe! Though I'm not sure I could have hacked it long term. Not only do I no longer drink, I also REALLY like being in bed by 10.30 p.m. these days.

So the long and the short of it was, I was paid for ideas. A dream come true. But also frankly terrifying to have to repeatedly have the light-bulb moment.

However, it did teach me a lot about the creative thinking process. One agency referred to it as 'circling' an idea. To me it feels a lot like unravelling a knot.

When you start musing on a concept you go round the houses, musing on all the whys and wherefores, only to often wind up back at the first thought. You could argue that going back and forth and interrogating all the other thoughts – sometimes for days at a time – was a waste of time. And it definitely might have felt like it. But by thinking around it you check that the idea is robust. That it's worth investing in.

Get better at trusting your instincts and knowing something

is a good thought. For me this still happens with Instagram – the posts that feel weird are often the ones that fly.

If in doubt I ask myself, is this thought based on a truth? Is it either amusing or educational? Better still, is it making me think about something in a different way?

Thinking about thinking is really uncomfortable. Not convinced? Start checking yourself when you go to wrangle a complex thought – do you opt out of the contemplating and fill it with a scroll through your phone or reach for a biscuit instead?

For me, thinking is like trying to untangle a bunched-up necklace. A tug here, a tug there. One bit seems to come away and make sense, but then one elsewhere is tighter or more snagged. If you keep going, little by little those necklaces will come loose again. And though it's tempting to shut them back in the drawer and ignore the tangle, that's way less satisfying than sorting the damn things out.

What else?

You know how your granny said *sleep on it*? She was wise. What feels like a monumental issue late at night can take on a whole new meaning when a) you are better rested, and b) your subconscious has done its thing. As well as sleeping on it, the walk away/delay technique is hugely valuable too.

It's hardly new news, is it? But it is worth remembering when wrestling with difficult subjects, and also when trying to connect with your child.

Sitting with a problem is actually brave and valuable. Also sitting with not knowing can take us from a place of reacting to a place of responding. Reacting is frequently emotional, based on a knee-jerk impulse. Allowing yourself to think properly comes from a place of conscious awareness, logic and calm.

Sit with the feelings. Think about thinking. There is a Buddhist saying that goes: 'If you let cloudy water settle, it will become clear. If you let your upset mind settle, your course will also become clear.' What a simple but powerful thing to remember.

As well as the benefits of circling round ideas (even if you end up coming back to the original one), another thing I learned to do in my advertising agency days was what was known as 'killing your baby', which is a horrendous expression. This essentially means you must be prepared to throw away a much-cherished idea or viewpoint if it turns out you made a mistake. When coming up with a good idea or figuring out your thoughts on stuff, it's vital to accept the possibility that you or it were wrong. Or that the idea you thought was great wasn't that great at all. Or indeed that there is a better one out there.

Accepting when you are wrong or when you have more to learn is huge. And vital. Going back to the quote at the beginning of this chapter: 'Normalise changing your opinion when presented with new information.' Normalise starting over as many times as you need. After all, progress never came from thinking the same thoughts. On the one hand, conversations with our kids are just conversations with kids. But on the other they are moments to push towards progress, albeit only incrementally.

Similarly, fact-check editor and journalist Lucinda Beaman's TED Talk 'What Does It Take to Change a Mind?'[27] reminds us to stop listening just to refute; instead listen to understand. Stop gunning for the other person to always be the one to change their mind.

Changing someone's mind about something is arduous; it takes patience, time, trust and respect. It takes skill and often a dose of kindness.

In light of that, it's worth considering, honestly, whether the person you are judging or trying to convert to your way of thinking is worthy of that investment.

But also be frank with yourself, while you are busy banging your head against the wall – perhaps it's *you* who needs to be more responsive. How open-minded are you really?

Beaman goes on to talk about how the amount of knowledge available at our fingertips is growing exponentially, but most of us aren't taking advantage of that because we are locked into our own viewpoint, even if we don't realise we are.

So when you hear, read or learn something – check in with your reaction. Think about what you are thinking. Think about it beyond the point that feels comfortable. Think about why it makes you uncomfortable. Think about how you came to that conclusion and why.

If in doubt, let that cloudy water settle. And if your kid asks you a question that you don't have an answer for, then the best tool in your armoury is: 'Let me think about that and get back to you.' Better a well-conceived response than a knee-jerk reaction. Just remember to get back to them later.

When I was a kid, I wish I had known that . . . everything was going to be okay. That I really didn't need to worry so much. That it was safe for me to let go and have fun and that it wasn't my responsibility to make sure everyone else was happy. When I was a kid, I wish I'd known how great and loveable I was.

Emma Campbell @limitless_em

5

QUESTIONS ABOUT
WORK AND MONEY

I enjoyed a stroll down memory lane with this one, remembering my first ever job as a babysitter: I must have been about fourteen and couldn't believe that you were allowed to help yourself to someone else's snacks as well as being paid!

This was followed by the joy of saving for a first purchase – Alanis Morisette's *Jagged Little Pill* album. The heady thrill of saving your own hard-earned cash for something you wanted!

Then there were many happy years as a waitress at Pizza Express. Probably the best job I ever had. Aside from the free pizza at every shift (see the food theme creeping in), I loved the fact you got to keep your own tips. Therefore the harder you worked, the more money you took home at the end of the shift. What an incentive! I was shamelessly goals-orientated even then. I soon learned if you said to a group of girls, 'Fancy sharing a couple of puddings, ladies?' they almost always went for it!

Lastly, I will never forget the day I got hired in advertising. The relief of finally feeling like I HAD A CAREER. Of course the career hasn't necessarily taken the shape I expected. But that afternoon it felt like my then boss, Trevor Beattie, had helped me onto the first rung of the ladder. Phew!

The working world has changed a lot since then: Generation Alpha are far less likely to work a career in the same way I thought I would. There is even a crazy statistic that suggests that most jobs our kids will have haven't even been invented yet! Which is mind-boggling – but then again, a podcaster and Instagrammer would have sounded like gobbledygook when I was twelve.

So the question is, how do we prepare our children for a working world that is more changeable than ever? And what are the wider lessons about money that underpin that? This chapter looks at some of these questions in more depth.

BUT WHY DOESN'T MONEY
GROW ON TREES?

You could, to an extent, argue that it does. Or more specifically that the paper version were made of trees, but of course it's more complicated than that; it always is!

Children often find it hard to understand the concept of money. This is especially the case given that we now live in a largely cashless society. In fact, according to The Youth Economy Report, Gen Z will almost always choose to go cashless, with only 14 per cent of six- to eighteen-year-olds' spending in cash.[28] As well as being the first digital natives, this generation is likely to be the first cashless natives too. The only time my kids actually see money is when the tooth fairy visits. And even then she's been known to renege on her responsibilities.

The question is, how do we make the concept of money less abstract? Even giving a dry explanation doesn't help much. A basic definition of money is 'anything that people use to buy goods and services'. It's what we get when we do stuff and what we give to other people when they do stuff or have stuff we want.

This is still very abstract for children. Chatting to Rachel Kerrone – head of brand for Starling Bank, mum of three and @parentmoney on Instagram – she suggested showing them your banking app. In the absence of getting money out of your wallet it's a great way to demonstrate money going in and out and the balance going up or down. It's important to puncture the illusion that we get things with the magic swipe of a card here or the tap of a phone there.

My first goal is to find a way to teach my kids about the ins and outs of how to use money sensibly, ideally in a way that is unemotional and unbiased. It's also important to be aware that our beliefs around money are formed early on. Here I spoke to Alice Olins, founder of Step Up Club, an organisation that helps women overcome professional obstacles. She explains: 'There is so much work we all have to do around our own money mindsets. We carry schemas and scripts into adulthood that we've learned as children, that we hear from the media, that we see in films and so on. These are our money stories and they often hold us back from earning what we're worth. How our parents talked about money (positive/negative), the school we went to, the affluence of our peers/friends, all of these and so many other external factors teach us a story about ourselves.' That can affect how we negotiate money in the workplace and in how we view the finances in our relationship, for example.

In her book *The Money Is Coming*,[29] Sarah Akwisombe gives an example of how often it's the emotions around money that children pick up on. 'Let's say your parents' beliefs were that you shouldn't use money for your own personal gain: that if you have left-over money you should give it to charity. You may have heard this spoken about as a youngster; maybe your mum and dad were having a quiet chat over dinner about their friends who had just splashed out on a new car when they "could have helped someone" with that money. At this young age, those thoughts aren't your own. But you recognise that your dad doesn't seem happy when he talks about his friends who were "selfish" with their money. You think he seems angry. Because you recognise the emotions that go along with it, you take that on board as something not to do. As a result, often the view of your parents (or whoever you grew up around) becomes your own.' This is regardless of the fact that your situation might be totally different, and of course as an adult you have the right to spend money as you see fit.

Given that attitudes to money are so inherited, it is important that we are conscious of our behaviours around it and reactions to it. Removing all emotion from finances is hard, because they are inextricably linked. But if we can empower our children with knowledge on how to navigate this stuff in a neutral manner then that's got to be a good starting point, hasn't it?

With this in mind, rather than work from a basis of my own thoughts around money, I thought it would be useful to throw the net wide. I asked my lovely audience on Instagram a couple of questions on this subject and their answers were fascinating and revealing. There were over 5,000 responses – here is a selection:

✳ What do you wish you had learned sooner about money? ✳

- It doesn't all need to be spent.

- That it's not everything.

- The importance of a good credit score.

- How tax works.

- That I didn't need to be quite so careful.

- How to budget because horrific debt is a vicious cycle.

- How important it is to save: something, anything. Always have a buffer. Sometimes the boiler and car go at the same time.

- The more you have, the more you spend.

- If you can't pay for it now, you won't pay for it later.

- That it comes and goes.

- How much of a deposit you need for a house and how a mortgage works.

- To always add VAT. And save 20 per cent.

- That it doesn't make you happy.

- There is no shame in not having it.

- Just because they will lend it to you, doesn't mean it is free money.

- How to budget.

My second question to Instagram was to ask people to complete the following sentence:

The greatest misunderstanding about money is . . .

- Your spending will have no consequences.

- That it's bad to have it and that it's bad to ask for more.

- That it fixes things.

- That payday loans help people: they don't.

- Compound interest and investment.

- That your wage reflects your value. And that it will increase year on year.

- That owning stuff doesn't actually mean freedom.

- That it's a taboo subject and shouldn't be spoken about. Why?!

- Perception about who has it: lots of everyday people who 'look rich' and buy big-ticket items are actually in debt.

- That you are lazy if you don't have it.

- That it doesn't need to be taught in schools.

- That it's fairly distributed.

- That if you have a lot you are greedy.

- Most common answer: that it will make you happy.

So many useful points there. When sifting through these responses and consulting the experts mentioned in this section, I found three recurrent themes: start the conversation early, learn by doing, and nothing comes for free. Let's look into each of those a little more in turn.

Start the money conversation early. Do your kids play shops? Do they beg you to buy something they neeeeedddd when out and about (e.g. snacks at the café or something from the dreaded magazine aisle)? If so, then they are old enough to start learning about money properly. I am not suggesting you try to explain interest rates to them when negotiating over why they can't have another pack of football cards, but research by the Money Advice Service reveals that children who are encouraged to talk about money, are given money regularly and are given responsibility for spending and saving tend to do better with money when they grow up.

Clare Seal is an interesting case in point. Author of *Real Life Money* and *The Real Life Money Journal*,[30] she has been documenting the process of working her way out of a £27,000 debt she accumulated simply by living month to month, with two pregnancies and a 'Pinterest-perfect wedding' which had caused her to lose her grip on her family's finances; essentially by living in denial.

I asked her what she's teaching her children to avoid the trap she fell in to. She replied, 'Our children are still quite young, but I feel like the earlier they're aware of the importance of money, the better. The key thing for me is to make sure they have the right balance – knowing that it's a brilliant tool, but not letting it define them. We're aiming to do this by talking openly about money – about spending it, saving it and being able to afford things.'

Which leads nicely into the next key point: **learning by doing**. Which is pretty self-explanatory. This might be as simple as getting your children to help you when you shop, either in person or online. Let them put things in baskets, pay for things, stay within a budget. Set a payment limit for a friend's birthday present and let them loose online and in store. Give them an idea of how far the dosh goes. If the budget doesn't allow, don't buy it. This is such a crucial lesson and one that we would all benefit from remembering.

Louise Hill, who founded the pocket-money card and app gohenry, is brilliantly matter-of-fact about it: 'There's no better way to learn the value of money than letting them buy that "must-have" item with their own money. They'll soon start to realise that things aren't as "must-have" as they originally thought when it's their own money that's gone.'

For Clare Seal, this principle has led her to give her son pocket money (loaded on a prepaid debit card) but also an earned allowance for doing tasks like tidying his bedroom and getting ready for school. 'If he wants to buy something more expensive, he knows that he needs to save up for a few weeks,' she says.

Rachel Kerrone from @parentmoney shared an idea run by her kids' school where each child was given £1 and asked to make it grow. The kids went to town organising cake sales and car washing. Not only was it a great education in regard to earning money, it also raised funds for the school. Could be a good one to suggest to your school?

Another idea is to have a 'kids in charge' day! This is my absolute fave, borrowed from art director and designer Emma

Scott-Child and her husband Tom. I know how much I would have LOVED this as a kid. It's got slight *Home Alone* vibes (but without the criminals and being deserted by your parents).

These are the rules. N.B. for reference they started doing this when their kids were six and nine and they always do it over a bank holiday weekend, so as to allow for 'recoup-eration' before school!

> *Welcome to two whole days where you are in charge! You can do whatever you want! From 7 a.m. on Saturday to 7 p.m. on Sunday you can go anywhere but you must look after yourselves and each other.*
>
> *You have £20 spending money (plus any pocket money you have saved).*
>
> *If you leave the house you MUST stay together. We will follow along behind but we won't help you.*
>
> *You must feed yourselves. There is plenty of food in the house, or you can buy your own, or cook if you want to.*
>
> *If you do anything stupid or dangerous, we will step in. And you MUST co-operate with each other.*
>
> *There will be no extension of screen time. You may borrow our phones if you want to:*
>
> *Make a phone call*
>
> *Look up something on a map*
>
> *Use Google*
>
> *GOOD LUCK! And don't forget that humans need food, water and sleep to live!*

Beyond these rules the kids can do what they like. Yes, it usually results in chocolate for breakfast and late nights. But it also teaches them that if they buy a load of magazines straight away they then won't have enough money for the taxi they desperately want to get later. It's fun, it's educational, and it also makes for relatively easy parenting. Winner!

Finally, there's one more important principle to teach children: that **nothing comes for free**. Now, all being well, the 'learning by doing' approach will have already made this clear. But it's definitely worth trying to make sure it has properly landed, by talking about how even things that you might not consider costing money do still need to be paid for. So, for example, take the pints of milk that they go through at an extraordinary rate – discuss paying the milkman in front of them. Talk about things you are saving for. Say: 'I am going to work now to earn money.' This is not about burdening; it's helping kids join the dots about how transactions occur. Additionally, explaining the difference between needs versus wants is a good way to do this. A *need* is a warm coat in winter. A *want* is a new Lego set or a trip to the zoo.

And as if all that wasn't enough to chew on, the brilliant Rachel Kerrone shared some additional pointers:

- Talk about why you work. That having a job means earning and getting paid. Show them visually how you get paid via your banking app or bank statement, and explain incomings vs outgoings.

- Give them pocket money, an allowance or money for helping with chores. Pocket money can be a regular weekly amount, or based on how helpful or well behaved they have been that week.

- Explain the basics of saving. For a five-year-old this may be a money box being gradually filled; for a fifteen-year-old a savings account that pays interest. Set savings goals then they have something to aim for. When they hit certain savings goals, perhaps offer to match what they have saved or add extra to show how interest on savings works.

- Saving in other ways is also a great lesson. Turning a light off saves electricity, buying something second hand saves money and the planet, taking a picnic saves money on bought lunches or fast food. Make these points regularly and they will soon become a habit.

- For older children, start explaining different financial products to them and put them into context. Tell them about mortgages, loans and credit cards. Use real-life examples of when you have saved for something, had to apply for a mortgage or loan, and what you looked out for.

- There are lots of apps out there specifically designed for children and all with a focus on financial education. For pocket money management and a personalised debit card try gohenry or RoosterMoney. For an account that gives children a debit card attached to their parents' current account, try Starling Bank Kite or Revolut Junior. There are lots of options from the high street banks too, but usually without the innovative features and child-friendly apps of the newer providers.

- Last but probably most importantly – give your kids the confidence to talk openly about money. Chatting to their friends about what they're saving for, how much pocket money they get, being proud of something they have worked for and earned.

It's a cliché but I wish this stuff had been taught in schools. Even as I approach the end of my thirties I feel I could and should know more. WAY MORE!

Clare Seal agrees: 'There's an infinite amount of improvement that needs to happen in our formal financial education to ensure that children and young people get off to the best start possible, but the missing piece really for me is context. It's entirely possible to know an absolute ton about money in a logical sense, but still be somehow unable to apply it to your real-life situation. We need to learn about value and worth alongside the more technical stuff, and about how money, or a lack of it, can impact our mental health and emotional wellbeing.' I couldn't agree more.

'So why doesn't money grow on trees?' Who are you kidding, sunshine? But it does make the world go round – which is why it's worth getting clued up. Indeed, as we head into more questions I do strongly recommend taking time to look at the work of the people who helped me with answers for this section, because they really are helping to shift the stigma and confusion about money, both for us adults and hopefully in turn for our kids.

Anyway, onwards.

BUT WHY CAN'T I HAVE A [INSERT MUST-HAVE ITEM]? EVERYONE ELSE HAS ONE!

I don't know about you but I find this to be an emotionally charged question because something in me wants to give my kids everything they want, but I know that isn't going to do them any good in the long run.

First up, remember that kids don't really 'get it'. Proof of their lack of understanding lies in two excellent conversations I had with my sons. One with Bertie who asked if I had ever had a thousand pounds.

His reaction to my confirmation that yes, indeed I had, was what you'd expect from someone who had just won the lottery. Mind well and truly blown. In that moment I was probably the wealthiest person he could possibly picture.

Secondly, I asked Woody where he fancied going one morning. We had a rare couple of hours for just the two of us, so wanted to do something lovely. 'I know . . .' he said, pausing. 'I would really like to go to South Africa.' Sky's the limit, my boy!

Wonderfully outlandish requests or sheer awe at the idea of possessing £1,000 shows that my boys have no concept of money (yet!). Much like when you ask kids to guess an adult's age, their ideas are just stabs in the dark. This means we should try to see their requests for 'must-have' items in the same spirit – as questions with no rational thinking behind them. So try not to let them wear away at you or make you feel guilty.

In fact, see this sort of request as a positive: it provides a great opportunity to put into practice some of the points from the previous questions – for example, explaining concepts like saving and budgeting.

I asked Alex Holder, author of *Open Up: The Power of Talking About Money*,[31] how she tackles this sort of question with her son. 'My son is four years old,' she says. 'He asks questions like "Can I have an ice cream?" and "Can I choose a magazine?" Sometimes they're not even questions, they're demands; he'll point at things and say, "I want that!" When I got upset because he'd drawn on my favourite top, he was confused. He told me to just "buy more, Mummy", like it was a box of cereal we'd run out of. All of these simple and everyday interactions require some understanding of money and resources. So I've been answering him honestly and explaining that while it appears that my card can pay for anything and that cashpoints look like they give you endless twenty-pound notes, money is finite. There isn't always enough money for everything we want. I talk to him about choices, that if we buy the magazine we can't also buy the balloon. That we can't have everything we see because it costs money. I also talk to him about the things money can't buy – a hug, a blue sky, that feeling when you hear a really funny joke.'

Again it comes back to the idea of budgets, and needs versus wants. They are the core pillars of what kids need to understand about 'wanting stuff'.

Depending on what it is they're asking for, consider the following:

- Tell them: 'If you still want it at your next birthday or Christmas we can put it on the list.' Kids are very faddy and may have gone off the item by that time, which is another reason not to drop the cash immediately. Delayed gratification is also good.

- Encourage them to save, and let them know how many weeks' worth of pocket money it will take. Find opportunities for them to add to the savings pot, e.g. by doing jobs or selling some things they no longer want.

- This could be a great way to show them the perks of second-hand shopping too.

- Help them understand the scale of the cost. A football kit is the same as ten packs of Pokémon cards.

- Remind them that friends who have the 'must-have' item probably did not magically just get it either. Maybe they share it with a sibling? Maybe it has just been their birthday or perhaps they have been saving.

And when you've talked through all of the above, maybe flip it over in your head. As a parent, I love being able to occasionally buy my kids the thing they really want. Especially if they have understood that it's something special. I remember the day I got my Game Boy – ahhh, I was on cloud nine, a big smile on my face as I got stuck into a marathon Tetris session!

BUT WHY AREN'T WE RICH?

Very good question, sweetheart! When people say you'd get bored if you won the lottery, I'm not sure I'd agree. I get the idea that we need purpose, but I would have a very good crack at having a pretty excellent time if I had a wedge of dosh in the bank.

I digress. The more mature and mindful retort to this question is: 'Rich in what?' Are we talking financially, emotionally, socially rich or something else?

Chances are, the kid asking this question imagines 'rich' in terms of material items. Or perhaps they have another idea in their head of what rich implies. So ask them! What does rich mean to them? Delve into their beliefs.

- Consider discussing whether they see themselves as fortunate.

- Is being rich having a certain amount of money?

- Do they feel like they are going without?

- This is an opportunity to make them understand the context of wealth around the world.

- Think about the language you use. 'Rich' and 'poor' imply a hierarchy. Rather than saying 'we are rich' or 'we are poor', say, 'We have to wait for what we want.' Usually you can't have things immediately; you have to save up.

Importantly, there is also an opportunity here to check in with what *you* think about wealth. Does rich look like Chanel handbags and multiple homes to you? (For me, it involves living in the sunshine – but I know I need to move on from that fantasy.)

Point is: is 'rich' something that is far away and unachievable? And if so, what would achieving it mean? I know better than to think being rich automatically means being happy. But it would also be unrealistic to pretend, for me at least, that money doesn't have a bearing on how content I am. Not because of what I can buy with it, but because being released from the stress that comes from needing it would certainly be liberating.

Personally, if being rich means having no financial worries and being poor means being consumed by them, we are fortunate to (currently) be somewhere in the middle. But even then, we're always conscious our circumstances might change: most people are only a few months or pay cheques away from being in financial difficulty. Having things just about 'ticking over' is a blessing.

I also threw out this question to Instagram. The most over-whelmingly common answer I was given from those I asked was along the lines of: 'We are rich in love.' Or: 'No, we are not but we have enough money. We are stable. We are com-fortable.'

One answer that stuck with me was: 'Yes, we are. Not because we have enough money to live well and have treats. We're rich because we are lucky. No, we're not poor, because we work hard. No, we're not poor, because we have each other. No, darling, our hearts are full and we have food in our bellies. We are full up. We aren't poor.'

The important thing here is to think beyond the idea of linking wealth only to money. There are so many other areas of poten-tial happiness: love, opportunity, fun, space. As Alice Olins, founder of Step Up Club, says: 'That definition of success – money, power, status – is so outdated now; we aren't "rich" or "successful" if we have a bulging bank balance, we're rich because we're happy, healthy, fulfilled and working to our purpose and values. The opposite, of course, is true of poverty.'

It is all relative. Young children have very little understanding of money but it's worth gently reminding your kids every so often that they are lucky and other people have harder lives than them. Not to scare them but just to help them understand that some of their friends may not have as much as they do – and hopefully to instill in them a desire to create a fairer world when they grow up.

Speaking to groups of people about their experience of growing up in poverty, a couple of their insights really stayed with me. One person remembered: 'Bailiffs at the door, Mum not eating meals to save money. Being cold, no heating at all.' Another respondent said: 'It's something that impacts you for the rest of your life; it's not something you ever move on from. My dad was in and out of work. I remember someone leaving an envelope of money on our porch on Christmas Day. I had an ongoing feeling of shame. I was bullied for living in a council house and shared a bedroom with my siblings – no personal space. I lived on an estate, so all my friends were in the same boat. But I don't remember going without.'

Poor might not look like how you think. One person said: 'Money mismanagement can mean a family can appear okay on the outside but the reality is different – it's happening down your road, under your nose. People's judgement is damaging. I was so aware of being looked down on because we were poor. I still feel poor, even though I am not any more; the anxiety remains. It can happen to anyone. The lack of money didn't bother me. The lack of opportunities did.'

And one final thing: several people mentioned that we should remember the global context. Yes, we are rich, because we are wealthier than 90 per cent of people in the world.

Key point: do not deny your kid's reality:

I received a message on Instagram that really stayed with me.

It read: 'Kids always, always know when it comes to the big stuff; denying or ignoring the reality is when the damage is done. Don't you think? So even when things were bad, we 1) were reassured that our interpretation was right, leading us to trust our judgement, 2) never felt totally powerless because knowledge is power, 3) didn't have to catastrophise (though mostly we did this anyway 😊) because we understood the situation fully, and 4) trusted our mum implicitly, which is incredibly important.'

Knowledge I hope to instill in my kids:

- Wealth is not a reflection of character.
- Never take things for granted.
- Know that you need to work hard.
- Understand how money works.
- Strip money away from the emotional attachment to it.
- Feel safe around money.
- Enjoy it, don't waste it.
- Have gratitude for what you do have.

Lastly, to go back to the original question, my favourite answer of all to 'But why aren't we rich?' was: 'We aren't rich *yet.*' I love the optimism of that, but also it's a reminder that money is changeable. Your financial status shouldn't stand in the way of your belief in yourself. And if money is where you find happiness, you'll always be poor.

BUT WHY DO YOU HAVE TO WORK?

Short answer: to earn money to buy stuff we want and need.

(Incidentally, when I answered this question from my boys, one of them said, 'What?! Someone gives you money just for looking at Instagram?' Ha! Good to know they have a great understanding of the career I have grafted to try and create . . .)

Longer answer: for structure, to give purpose. In some industries it might even be linked with self-expression or helping others.

When I told my kids that one day they would get a job, probably around the age of eighteen (that's the average age to get a first job in the UK, up from sixteen a decade ago), they were absolutely blown away. But before that, many children are already earning. According to The Youth Economy Report, British children and teenagers aged six to eighteen collectively earned £4.5 billion in 2018. This income came from pocket money and ad-hoc gifts, plus payments for undertaking informal household chores, such as tidying their room, washing the dishes, doing homework and brushing teeth. Walking the dog earned the highest 'wage' (£1.50), along with good behaviour (£1.45) and tidying their room (£1.40). Chores which paid the least include setting the table (£0.70), making the bed (£0.80) and brushing teeth (£0.80). Fascinating!

But what can we learn from our first experiences of proper employment? Throwing out the research on Instagram, it seems most people think favourably on their own early jobs. They remember the feeling of independence, of purpose and of having achieved something. Having money meant they 'felt like they were contributing' or simply 'had more phone credit'. And of course there was the impact on how employment makes you feel in yourself: 'I felt grown-up,' said one person. 'It did wonders for my self-esteem,' remembered another.

And many mentioned fun! It's easy to forget that, isn't it? Work can be fun. And on the flip side, the absence of work can be really tough (more on that in a moment).

Listening to TV personality Scarlett Moffatt in Elizabeth Day's *How to Fail* podcast, she initially frames having multiple jobs as a failure. But on closer consideration, she changes her mind: a work ethic and a commitment to always having a job shows an entrepreneurial spirit and a good deal of resilience. I think that's true!

How do we translate all that into how to answer the question of why people work?

- Consider throwing the question back at them! From there, it's easy to ask kids what they think they might want to do. There is joy in hearing what small humans want to be when they grow up. (I wanted to be a vet for many years, until it became apparent that I neither enjoyed nor was very good at science – apart from the bit where you could burn stuff with a Bunsen burner.)

- Chat about the things that a job gives you: a sense of reward or fun, satisfaction, making a difference.

- Teach them that sometimes you do have to do jobs you don't love, because working is necessary to earn money, to buy food and to pay to live somewhere.

Also, this is so obvious, but actually a useful part of the conversation: do your kids know what you do? Apart from the 'getting paid for looking at Instagram' comment, I think my kids also know that I do some sort of writing. So that's a start.

Growing up, I was pretty clueless: my dad commuted to London from Leighton Buzzard throughout my childhood and for a long time I thought his office was on the train. (In fact, he is a barrister.)

There is a lot to be gained from kids really understanding what you do in your work. What tasks do you do? What do you enjoy about it? How did you get the job?

Showing them what you do or even bringing them into work is not only useful for answering questions, but it also helps give clarity when you say you are working.

For example, when I got asked, 'Why aren't you coming to the park again, Mummy?', I gave them the truth: 'I can't come because I need to write 800 words for the book.'

'Wow! That's a lot of words,' was the reply and instantly they seemed to 'get' why I needed to hide away tapping at my keyboard. And even better, when they then came home and asked how many words I had written, it felt like a little boost of encouragement. Win-win!

What else? There is a lot to pack in here.

I picked the brains of three experts (who are also parents) for advice: Alice Olins, founder of Step Up Club, HR consultant Jessica Jones and journalist Anna Whitehouse, founder of the flexible working campaign Flex Appeal.

After chatting to them and going back through the archives of Mother of All Lists, which has featured stories from people whose careers range from abortion nurse through to air steward and even news presenter, I pulled together a bunch of insights that might inform a response to the question.

- Work looks different for everyone.

- Work is never a measure of anyone's value – including your own.

- Nobody is better or worse than someone else because of the job they do.

- If a job is worth doing, it is worth doing well.

- Work can be hard work, but that doesn't make it bad. So often the 'why on earth am I doing this?' moments are promptly followed by 'yay! I'm so glad I did that!' ones.

- You don't have to love work every day. But neither should you endure something that makes you unhappy.

- Help other people out. (Remember how it felt to be given a chance or shown how to use the photocopier on your first day – do that for those on their way up.)

- Don't dig up in doubt what you planted in good faith. We all have phases where we want to jack it all in and run away to the sun. Number one, that isn't realistic. Number two, bad patches are just that; sometimes you've got to stick 'em out!

- There is a lot of truth in Steve Jobs' philosophy of trying not to overthink things and instead allowing the dots to join. That can include hobbies, random meetings, one-off gigs. There will be times when it feels disconnected, but so often the disconnected things find their way of becoming an actual thing. In Jobs' case, that thing was Apple! But who knows what brilliant thing your seemingly random bits might become?

- And, to throw a total spanner in the works, some of the most important jobs aren't paid at all (more of this in the next section).

In answer to the original question, people want different things from work. Not all of it is about money; some care about the type of work, the community they work with, the benefits, the prestige, the ability to work from home, the travel . . .

In a *Vogue* article entitled 'What 9 Parents Tell Their Kids About Why They Go to Work',[32] one respondent spoke of splitting their response into two parts: the economic reason to work and the 'additional' or personal reasons.

One parent in the article also made a point of telling her daughter that she enjoys her work. For me it's about being realistic: work is necessary, we do it to pay the bills, sometimes it's hard, often it can be really satisfying, ultimately it's a privilege.

A note on unemployment:

As I write this, I am all too aware that although Covid has been a health crisis, the long-term impact will be an economic one. It got me thinking about if and how we should be talking to kids about *not* working.

For context, I wanted a better understanding of what different experiences of unemployment felt like. I asked 2,000 people if they had ever been made redundant/unable to work. Thirty-seven per cent had, and their descriptions of how it felt were vivid: *'Confidence-shattering . . . Painful . . . Liberating . . . It happened when I was quite young so saw it as an opportunity . . . Scary . . . Lucrative . . . Depressing . . . More upsetting than I was expecting, despite a decent payout . . . Huge sense of rejection . . . I felt embarrassed and ashamed . . . Utterly humiliating . . . First redundancy was a shock and a life lesson; the second I was better prepared but still it shattered my confidence . . . Demoralising . . . Turned out to be the best thing that ever happened to me.'*

What these answers revealed is that not being able to work is (unsurprisingly) tough; partly because, as we have already established, work is linked to our sense of self, but also because it gives us purpose, which can be fundamental to our mental health. Also of course, there is the stress of the financial insecurity.

Redundancy isn't necessarily a bad thing. Some saw it as a turning point or a relief. However, I might suggest that is only something you can know with the benefit of hindsight. Much of it depends on the circumstances. In many cases it's not something you have a choice in, which limits our sense of independence. It also depends on how vulnerable you are at the time (for example, I am thinking of redundancy during pregnancy here) and what your future prospects are.

The next challenge is how do you explain it to the kids? First it's important to acknowledge how tricky this is. One question to consider is how long term you think the period of unemployment will be, as that might shape how much information you give. The general consensus seemed to be to keep it simple and honest; for example: 'There are not enough jobs at the moment', or 'This is a time between jobs', or 'This was just some bad luck'. This makes sense to me, as does avoiding equating unemployment with not getting money. Stick to just saying you're not working and leave it at that.

Invite questions from them. Avoid defaulting to false positives and keep things factual. For yourself and them, remember that it will end, and that it's nobody's fault. This is a moment, not something that defines you or your family.

Working is a gift. Jessica Jones put it brilliantly: 'Working can teach you practical life skills such as time management, responsibility and communication. It looks different for everyone. It doesn't need to be boring – you can love your job and should strive to work in a career you are passionate about.'

Ask your children what they want to be when they grow up. It's a brilliant opportunity to delve into their ambitions and ideas of work and also maybe something great to remind them of when they head off into a career decades later.

BUT WHY DOESN'T DADDY WORK?

The answer in our family is simple. 'Daddy does have a job and it's a brilliant one: Daddy takes care of you lot!'

Anyone who has been the primary childcare provider will know, without a shadow of a doubt, how challenging, exhausting and relentless that role is.

Not only that, but the work done at home, raising the next generation, is in my opinion the work that helps shape the future of society and indeed the workforce of tomorrow. As the William Wallace poem says: 'The hand that rocks the cradle is the hand that rules the world.'

When I spoke to Caitlin Moran off the back of her book *More Than a Woman*,[33] she spoke about how if the last ten years were about lobbying for self-love, the next decade would be about the need for appreciation and indeed pay for the unseen work that goes on behind closed doors – caring for elderly relatives, nurturing children, tending to those who are sick or mentally unwell. These are the tasks that keep society functioning. These are the roles that deserve recognition and support and remuneration.

Penny Wincer has written extensively, including in her first book, *Tender*,[34] and here in an extract from Mother of All Lists, about her role as a carer both to her mother, a role she took on from the age of fourteen, and later to her son Arthur, who is autistic, and his younger sister. She says:

- Being a carer is not always what people might think it means. Many people assume caring is all about personal care – bathing, dressing, feeding. But though that is often part of it, it can be far more complex than that.

- Carers are legal advocates, medical care co-ordinators, physical and occupational therapists, speech therapists, play therapists, cooks, drivers, companions and much more. It is far more than the time you spend in the physical presence of the person you support.

- There are around 7 million unpaid carers in the UK at any one time. Carer's Allowance, the benefit that you can claim if you care for someone more than thirty-five hours per week, is £67 per week. It is the lowest of all benefits in the UK. Eight out of ten carers feel lonely or isolated as a result of their caring role.

- Overall, 58 per cent of carers are women but that rises to 72 per cent for those who are caring more than thirty-five hours per week. Anxiety levels in carers are twice as high as in the general population.

- What most carers say they need is more regular breaks from caring. The next most important thing for carers is more understanding from society. Carers are paying too high a price, in terms of their emotional and physical health, as well as in lost earnings, for the unpaid work they do.

A sobering and important read if ever there was one. It offers a great example of possible answers to the question of why someone might not work, whether it's because they're a stay-at-home parent with young children or whether they're looking after someone elderly or with special needs.

Though we know how important these caring roles are, they are all too often overlooked, something that Nicola Washington, teacher, digital media manager and mother of two, captures perfectly in this piece she originally wrote for a live event I hosted. It's called 'Work-Life Balance? Not Me'[35] and I think and talk about it often. Here's an excerpt:

- If you are a parent, you will probably be familiar with the death-by-a-thousand-paper-cuts nature of looking after small children. You might also know that when you become a full-time carer, it becomes clear that while most people accept it is hard, very few will see it as work.

- It turns out that I was one of them.

- In my head I wasn't doing anything. Or at least, nothing I was doing had any value, and I wanted to get back to work – proper work, paid work.

- My cultural conditioning insisted that real work is accompanied by a pay cheque. The many hours of unpaid labour that take place in the home – the domestic burden – do not count.

- To add insult to injury, organising our lives into a tussle between just two opposing forces of work and life means that if the domestic burden is not work, it therefore must be life.

- It is essential to our humanity to maintain space between the mundane daily tasks that are part of life-with-a-small-l that keep us alive, and the Life-with-a-big-L pursuits that make us feel alive.

- But the work of wiping noses, bums and floors disguises itself as Life-with-a-big-L and this posed a problem for me. I wasn't working, so why wasn't I happy to be living? I dripped bitter tears while condemning my selfish sense of entitlement – how could I want more when I apparently already had so much?

- But perhaps the problem was never me. The deficiency was not in my character – it was an error in the equation of work-life balance.

- Work-life balance has long been seen as the route to emotional, mental and physical wellbeing, but in fact it has never been possible to divide life into two neat halves. Although starved of attention, there has always been a third appetite equally hungry for our time, but if you can't see it, how can you value it?

- Lifting unpaid labour out of my peripheral vision and into plain sight attributed it with the importance it had always deserved. Rather than lurking in the underbelly of my life and mind, the domestic load now co-exists, fully acknowledged, alongside the importance of paid employment.

- And importantly, never again will I confuse taking care of my children's lives for living my own.

This is a fraction of Nic's list. I urge you to read the rest and also to keep in mind that the most important roles are the ones that often go unseen, but absolutely shouldn't go unappreciated.

JOINING BIT FIVE:

HONESTY ALWAYS
(OR NEARLY ALWAYS)

Honesty is the first chapter in the book of wisdom.
Thomas Jefferson

I am a huge advocate of honesty; I think it has the power to be really transformative, but it is a complex and nuanced subject so indulge me while I talk around it a little.

For me, honesty means a couple of things:

- Being honest with yourself is often the first step towards progress.

- You need to be honest about life and its struggles.

Yes, I know the notion of 'life and its struggles' appears bleak and very glass-half-empty. I believe in honesty grounded in realism. Life isn't fair. You can't get everything you want. Good things happen to bad people. That can sound hugely depressing, but in fact there is something very liberating in realising this.

For me, realism breeds gratitude. It doesn't quash dreams but it does set expectations. Expectations that can be beaten outweigh dashed hopes.

The Stoics were champions of realism. And when I spoke to philosopher Alain de Botton he felt inspired by the notion of avoiding trying to protect our kids too much and painting the world to be an easy, breezy ride. If we do that, at best we are doing them a great disservice and at worst we are setting them up for a fall.

For example, as a kid I had to face the disappointing realisation that I am musically challenged. I'll explain. I am one of five siblings. Three out of five of us can sing; one does so professionally. I am one of the two that can't. And yes it was a sucker-punch realisation that my singing along to 'Summer Nights' (*Grease*, obvs) was a horrendous caterwaul, rather than the pitch-perfect rendition I heard in my head. But better to receive the blow of that knowledge at home than being confronted with it in the real world in the misplaced belief that I had the voice of an angel.

This isn't about raining on anyone's parade. However, the honest realist in me thinks that getting used to the idea that things don't always go our way is vital. The fact is, failure isn't pleasant but it is utterly unavoidable. Yet rather than teach this fact gently, there is often an attempt to remove any possibility of failure completely.

Take the classic game, pass the parcel. When I was a kid we all got to have a go at unwrapping a layer, but there was only one winner: the person who discovered the prize inside the last layer (much to the envy of the rest of us). Not any more. These days, everyone wins at pass the parcel. The 'done thing' is to put a prize under every single layer, thus circumnavigating any disappointment amongst the participants. Sweet idea, good intention, but it's a small example of how we have lost the opportunity to build resilience.

The 'kind optimist' might say to the tone-deaf child: 'Sure, go ahead and follow your dreams – go audition for *The X Factor*.' But isn't it kinder to say, 'Sure, keep singing in the shower,' but encourage them to focus their dreams elsewhere?

I have a huge bunch of British wild flowers tattooed on my inner arm. When asked about them I could tell the kids that they are there because they are pretty, but the honest answer is they are a reminder of a challenging time in my past. I used to say, 'No rain, no flowers,' over and over in my head. Sometimes we have to go through the tough bits, the boring bits, the grey bits, the disappointing bits, but when we do, and the rewards pay off and the sun comes out, the flowers bloom and we achieve something.

Kids are blessed with honesty:

'Mummy, why do you look SO old?'

This was the opening gambit from my middle son on Face-Time one Friday night during the summer holidays. While he had been at his grandparents', I had been doing a series of long days to hit deadlines. Admittedly it wasn't what I wanted to hear, but ego aside, the important thing is that his observation was just an observation. There was no mean intention; how I chose to process it was up to me.

We should respect our children and apply that honesty in return.

I don't advocate burdening kids, but do them the service of being truthful. Psychologist Nicole LePera (@the.holistic. psychologist) explains how avoiding the truth with children can come from wanting to protect them, but having their reality denied can be damaging. If the child is seeing or experiencing something different, then our denial invalidates their feelings and intuition.

So we need to resist the urge to make the tough stuff disappear. It's something I was interested in in relation to Ben Tansley, who was paralysed in a motorbike accident. What did he teach his children about this experience? I asked.

'I have always tried to teach my kids the value of life,' he replied, 'not the value of things, as these do not make you happy. Yes, they give us short periods of joy, but they won't provide the key to happiness long term. So having my accident was a sure way of teaching them the importance of living a life true to yourself, because at the best of times it's short and if you do stumble upon some bad health it can be even shorter, so you should always do what makes you happy and not wait too long to do it.'

Ben went on to say that a grounding principle for him is that although you can't control everything that happens to you, you can control your attitude towards it and how you deal with it – and that's exactly it, isn't it?

Something like a terrible accident or a death – or indeed a birth – are huge shifts, but they are also gifts because they strip everything back, give you a rare dose of perspective and help you understand what's actually important.

We have all got caught up in this false idea that life should look and feel like a pretty pastel-hued Instagram filter all the time. Let's move away from a need for glittery optimism and curated perfection and be more connected to spotting the joy on what might appear to be an average day.

Take those Saturdays with no plans that initially feel a bit disappointing but then, because you have no expectations, the day ends up being amazing – you go to the park, bump into friends, end up grabbing a takeaway pizza and hanging out right up until bedtime. The reason it's so special is because you didn't have preconceived ideas of how it should be, and instead enjoyed how it was.

So how do we get more honest? And not be tempted to construct our lives or indeed our kids' childhoods through an Instagram filter?

Learning to be honest:

Here are some ideas for increasing the chances of honesty being useful rather than something to be feared:

- Check in on the intention of the honesty. If its sole motive is unkindness then forget it.

- Honesty needs to be based on context – your relationship, the subject you are talking about, where you both are at.

- Honesty involves boundaries. Everyone's boundaries are different. And everyone is in a different place with regard to their exposure to honesty (and vulnerability). Give people the option to say, 'Not today.'

- Honesty requires self-compassion. Recently I had the opportunity for an honest conversation in relation to body image, but at the time my mental health was in a shady patch. And so I wasn't resilient enough. That's okay. That isn't a cop-out. That is being mindful of the context of honesty.

- Honesty requires emotional intelligence.

- Honesty can take time. Don't be honest with someone if the relationship is for the short haul (probably why throwaway comments on social media feel wrong).

- Honesty should not be used to win a power struggle or for personal gain. This isn't about proving a point or ensuring an outcome.

- Honesty shouldn't come with an assumed reaction or outcome.

- Honesty is truthful but not unfiltered. It stems from respect.

- Honesty works both ways. Don't dish it out if you aren't

prepared to receive it in return. You also have to be okay with not swaying the other person to your way of thinking. And you even have to be okay with someone not liking you. For me, a natural people-pleaser, I find that so uncomfortable. But I'd love my kids to be all right with not being liked from the off.

· If the honesty you receive is appreciated, tell them. I feel inclined to say thank you for honesty, because to me it is an opportunity to see things outside of myself and often it is a chance to grow (or consciously stay as I am).

When questioning if honesty is the right thing in a given situation, I ask myself: what is the consequence of *not* being honest? And I weigh that up and compare it to the likely outcome of sharing a truth.

The word 'honesty' is loaded. We assume that the only brand of honesty is 'brutal honesty', which is explosive and focused on uncomfortable truths delivered with little care for their impact.

But honesty is also about having meaningful conversations, and sharing truths. It's being authentic and sharing your thoughts because you trust the other person. Honesty is the antithesis of people-pleasing or easy chit-chat and saying what people want to hear.

I hope life is forever sunny for my kids, but if it is not, then telling them they might need wellies and a brolly along the way is the least I can do. No rain, no flowers. Or rainbows. And as poet Henry Wadsworth Longfellow said: 'The best thing one can do when it is raining, is let it rain.'

When I was a kid, I wish I had known that . . .
being a grown-up is wonderful because you can
make your home safe and happy and exactly as
you wish it to be. Being academic isn't the most
important thing in the world beyond school
because your kindness and your energy are so
important but there is no exam for that. However, exams and trying hard at school are good
because they teach you how to do things you
might find hard (like a really tricky presenta-
tion at work). Money won't make you a happy
person – that's something that comes from
inside you – but taking care of your money, and
learning about it, is a really important thing.
The world sends out lots of messages about
what a woman is meant to be – through films
and telly and magazines and chatter – but you
get to decide who you are. You are a beautiful,
strong, interesting woman – no matter what
anyone tells you. ONLY YOU gets to decide
who you are. The only thing that matters is
that you love the amazing, unique miracle that
you are.

Cherry Healey @cherryhealey

6

MISCELLANEOUS QUESTIONS

In the BBC drama *I May Destroy You*, there is a scene where Michaela Coel covers the wall with Post-it notes, unpicking the structure of her book. There were several moments exactly like this for me during this process, and one of the main sticking points was trying to sort questions into neat subcategories. There is so much crossover between complex feelings, health and body image, the 'big wide world' and our relationships. No surprise really – and increasingly as I wrote, I found that I learned approaches to answering questions that would transcend the subject and instead cement my values. I hope you are finding that to be the case too.

It also taught me to be less rigid in general.

My default is to be quite black and white – if I can sort things into convenient categories, that works for me. But that isn't always realistic or indeed even helpful. So instead we find ourselves with a section called 'Miscellaneous Questions', which on the one hand is very vague, but on the other hand reminds us that random is so blooming important too.

BUT WHYYYYYYY CAN'T I HAVE
AN ICE CREAM (PLEEEASE)?

The answer to this probably stems from an awareness that too much sugar isn't a great thing. For me it's also linked to the fact that I am horrified that a 99 Flake from an ice cream van now costs close to £2.50 (or it does at Peckham Rye Park). What an absolute joke. (Insert classic old-person comment along the lines of 'when I was a kid . . .' or 'what is the world coming to . . . ?')

First up and by way of a seamless segue, I want to acknowledge that educating kids about food ain't no walk in the park. What can be one of life's simple pleasures is also hugely complicated.

NHS surgical doctor, Instagrammer and *Cut Through Nutrition* podcaster Dr Joshua Wolrich posted something that really reminded me to look at the big picture. He said: 'Food is so impacted by our socioeconomic status, our privilege, our preference, our choices, where we live, what we have grown up with on top of that.' In particular, he pointed to research on food inequality: 'The poorest 10 per cent of UK households would need to spend 74 per cent of their disposable income on food to meet the Eatwell Guide costs. This compares to the richest 10 per cent only having to spend 6 per cent. Stereotypically "unhealthy" (high in fat, salt and/or sugar) foods are three times cheaper than "healthy" foods per kcal.'

He goes on: 'Over 1.2 million people in the UK live in what are known as "food deserts", areas of food insecurity where poverty, poor public transport and lack of big supermarkets severely limit access to affordable fresh fruit and vegetables. Almost 4 million children in the UK live in households that struggle to afford/access fresh fruit and vegetables. One million people in the UK are living without a fridge. Two million are without a cooker and 3 million without a freezer.'[36]

Food is complex, on every level.

It's such a fundamental need and it is deeply emotive. As such, answering the questions with facts should render the conversation easy. Except it doesn't. Conversations around food – in particular its relationship with health and obesity – are political, and mealtimes are stressful for most parents. And being asked for a snack 576 times a day (or indeed an ice cream every time you go to the park, even in February) can and will send you bonkers.

Also, though we might like to be whipping up varied and exquisite culinary delights for our children on a regular basis, it's just not realistic. I am not looking for an easy way out, but more of a reality check. Three kids, three different eaters with varying degrees of fussiness, and on really bad days there will be times when they each hate at least one (different) component of the meal. Or they'll agree on eating pasta but be adamant that they each want a different sauce because one of the sauces is disgusting, despite it having been their very favourite the previous week, obviously.

And have you noticed how, the more effort you put into making them something nice, the more likely they are to reject it? Sod's bloody law.

I am not alone in finding it all a challenge. I asked Instagram 'what are the hardest things about teaching kids about food?' and I received 500 answers!

Far and away the most common response was finding a balance when it comes to discussing food with children. **How** do you encourage healthy habits without causing unhealthy behaviours?

Other concerns were: how to encourage them to try new things; how to avoid them becoming fussy eaters and what to do once they had already become picky; and how to stop them eating the same thing over and over or to move towards greater variety. There was also a repeated concern about the food waste that comes with kids refusing to eat, which only added to the sense of guilt around mealtimes. I hate food waste; it gives me the fear. It's depressing. All of these are relatable problems, or to me at least, so as such we will work our way through some solutions shortly.

Also, there appeared to be A LOT of concern about food information coming from outside sources, in particular grandparents having conflicting or seemingly outdated views. Similarly, schools sometimes put out different messaging around food compared to home.

For me there are a few options when it comes to dealing with this last concern. Firstly, if it's possible to talk to the school or the grandparents, do. Though remember to have a level of tolerance of other people's ideas; not everyone has the same education or ideas you do. There isn't a 'one size fits all' way to feed kids.

Alternatively, accept it for what it is and instead focus on what you CAN do in terms of landing a consistent and considered approach.

The last common concern in regard to teaching kids about food was about teaching 'moderation'. How do we get them to stop eating when they are full? There is an answer: it's called eating intuitively and kids do it naturally. I know this to be true. Sometimes my kids will eat breakfast for what feels like hours: bowl after bowl of cereal. Then the following week they will eat next to nothing. Then just as I start to worry that they will never eat again, they go back to the continual consumption of something else. These 'up and down' eating habits can feel uncomfortable, especially if you are conditioned to eat certain things and certain amounts of things at specific times. I am so used to having two pieces of toast with Marmite on a Saturday that I rarely stop to consider whether I'm in the mood for a third slice or whether perhaps one would suffice.

We adults teach intuition out of kids. 'Don't force a child to clean their plate,' says Laura Thomas PhD. Laura works at the London Centre for Intuitive Eating and is the author of *Just Eat It*,[37] which fundamentally shifted my relationship with food. She goes on to say that by focusing on clean plates we are teaching kids to override their fullness signals, which 'undermines the trust they have in their bodies to know how much they need to eat. Kids' appetites can fluctuate enormously from day to day and week to week, so take a step back and notice their overall growth patterns.'

This is a great starting point. What else is there to think about in relation to how we talk to kids about food? For this I looked to a few key sources: Laura Thomas; Susie Cunningham, a therapeutic wellbeing practitioner with fourteen years' experience working with children at risk of exclusion through cooking and eating with them (and also my sister); and Jennifer Anderson's amazing Instagram, account @kids.eat.in.color, a brilliant source of straightforward advice.

The key insights I got from them and other reading around the subject are: **eat together, get them involved, keep it relaxed, stick with it, don't divide foods into 'good' and 'bad'.** Let's take each one in turn:

First of all, **eat with them**, ideally as a family. Or even just sit with them while they eat. Jennifer Anderson of Kids Eat in Color goes so far as saying that you being there with them at mealtimes has more influence on their eating habits than what you serve them.

Sitting down for a meal with friends is absolutely one of my favourite things to do in the whole world (remember when that was something we did pre-Covid)? How are my kids going to learn if we don't start showing them that food is sociable? Also, it's a great time to throw about ideas or difficult questions and have those honest chats, or teach them about where food comes from. To be clear, we achieve this rarely during the week but we do make it a priority at weekends.

Get them involved. When kids are involved in cooking, they are more likely to eat what is made. Also it's a great life skill.

One of the few perks of the first lockdown was that mine learned to cook perfect scrambled eggs. Sure, it was quite a messy educational process. However, it does mean they can now make a very basic meal for themselves.

During the actual mealtime, **give them as much autonomy as possible.** Go buffet-style and let them help themselves. When mine ask me, 'How many vegetables do I have to have?', I throw it back to them: 'Take an amount that you think is appropriate.' They nearly always put more than I expect and are more likely to eat them all because there's a bit of choice involved. It's not failsafe, but it's worth a go.

What else? **Keep it relaxed.**

Chill, chill, chill. They will pick up on any stress. Mealtimes that are a battle are no fun for anyone. Laura Thomas says, 'Avoid pressure – if you have a "fussy" or "faddy" kid, or one who doesn't seem all that interested in eating their veggies, it's tempting to want to encourage them to have a few more bites, or "just one mouthful for Mummy". This might work in the moment, but long term it's likely to make a little one more anxious and apprehensive about mealtimes – think about when you are forced to do something you don't want to do; it can be stressful, right?

'Research shows that putting pressure on kids to finish their plate or eat a few more bites can ultimately contribute to more pickiness. When they go on a carrot strike, try not to freak out and keep offering them alongside foods you know they will eat, even if that means smothering the carrots in ketchup! It can also be helpful to sit down and eat the carrots with them – for example, if they're having some with dinner at 5 p.m., can you have some with hummus for a snack? Setting an example goes a long way in helping kids learn to enjoy foods.'

Stick with it.

I have often laughed to myself about the token slice of cucumber on the side of a slice of pizza or the token piece of broccoli. But as Jennifer @kids.eat.in.color says, seeing something often will increase the chances of them eating it.

What if your child suddenly develops an aversion to something they'd previously accepted? Laura Thomas explains: 'Food neophobia – a scepticism of foods – is a normal developmental stage that means kids might go off their favourite food overnight.' We all know how frustrating this can be and the obvious quick-fix solution is to give up and swap in a failsafe option (pasta and bread, in our house). Laura recommends resisting temptation and, if you can, try not to react, and keep offering the food as part of their meals and snacks, otherwise it can become a self-fulfilling prophecy. Even if it's three peas on a plateful of macaroni cheese, keep offering.

In a similar vein, when it comes to variety, a simple hack that works for us is trying new stuff on a Saturday lunch. Firstly, it's a time when we are eating together so they see us eating it, but secondly and more importantly, they are more chilled. By comparison, on a weeknight after school, everyone is tired, which automatically equals far less chance of success. (And by 'far less', I mean zero chance.)

Make introducing new foods fun. The government recommends ten portions of fruit and veg a day. Ten! That feels overwhelming, whereas 'eat the rainbow' feels nicer.

And finally, this is the big one: most nutritionists will tell you not to put certain foods on a pedestal. No 'good' and 'bad' food. 'When we use words like "treats", "naughties" or "unhealthy", we might inadvertently be making them more exciting and interesting to kids, which of course makes them want them more!' explains Laura Thomas. Plus of course there is an impact at the opposite end of the scale too. Using these words 'has the effect of making other foods seem yucky and gross by comparison. It's like saying that you have to eat this icky broccoli to get the ice cream prize at the end. When we treat all foods neutrally, it levels the playing field so that broccoli and ice cream are equal; neither is better or worse than the other, they're just foods.'

Makes sense to me, but you'd be surprised how ingrained some of these messages are. I know I still sometimes think to myself that as I've had a shit day I *deserve* to inhale half a bar of Tony's Chocolonely (have you tried it? Boy, it's delicious). The action of enjoying the bar isn't problematic in itself, but framing it as a treat could be. Instead I can just have some chocolate because I fancy it.

Which brings me nicely back to the question in hand: 'but why can't I have an ice cream?'

This might be a place where you want to talk to kids about sugar. If so, Jennifer Anderson is quick to point out that it's important to steer clear of the 'sugar is poison' territory. Black and white thinking does not take account of the nuances of the subject and instead could veer into scaremongering.

Instead, she points out that the World Health Organization recommends we reduce our added sugar to no more than 10 per cent and ideally less than 5 per cent of total energy intake, which is roughly 25g (six teaspoons) of sugar.

Be aware of, but don't be obsessive about, the sugar your kid is consuming. As a handy way of thinking about it, perhaps take Susie Cunningham's approach: 'I see sugar a little as I see TV: try to avoid it for as long as you can, but let it happen eventually. If you avoid it altogether you could potentially deny your child being part of their cultural landscape and make them want it even more. In our cooking groups, we made the decision to use sugar when appropriate. We know it's a part of children's lives and we know in moderation it's a true treat and forms part of all our childhood food memories.'

Drawing on the idea of 'showing rather than telling' kids, Susie takes this approach: 'If we are making a cupcake or lemonade, we show children how much sugar goes into it; teach this way first. Then we experiment with alternatives like making the lemonade with honey and comparing it with the sugar version. We have even had sessions comparing the taste with a shop-bought lemonade. You'll be amazed at the preferences children have around their own creations purely because they've been involved in the process.'

'Avoid being the sugar police,' adds Laura Thomas. 'We all want our kids to grow up being healthy and eating a varied and balanced diet. We also hear lots of (super unhelpful) messages about sugar being "poison" or "addictive". That means that sensible messages to be mindful of how much sugar our kids eat get misconstrued as "kids shouldn't have any sugar". Having an all-out ban on sugar can backfire by making kids obsessed with the stuff – this is also known as the forbidden fruit effect. If we never expose kids to sweet foods then they never learn how to manage them competently. Again, role modelling a healthy balance with sweets can be helpful here – give kids regular access to them, without making them a big deal.'

Be mindful of where the sugar is coming from. I don't think the problem lies in us using sugar when we cook at home. It's what we buy when we are out or in the shops – the (mass) consumerism around sugar. So our approach should be to get children into the kitchen, engage in a debate with them and make it an opportunity for learning together, and hopefully reaching a healthy relationship with sugar.

Possible answers in relation to sugar (or any other food) being bad:

- Sugar isn't bad, though too much of it can have some less good outcomes. It can decay your teeth, plus when we look at the types of foods that are high in added sugar, they often are not high in nutrition, so they don't necessarily fill you up (or help your hunger). And sugar can lead to cravings, which trick you into thinking you want more, even if you don't really.

- Too much of anything is bad.

- Consider talking about food in terms of fuel – fats give you energy; protein builds up your muscles; vitamins and minerals in fruit and vegetables help your body work in the best way possible; fibre helps your poo come out smoothly; sweet things like sugar also give you energy, but as long as you're eating loads of colourful vegetables too, your body will be happy.

- Explain why it's good to eat a rainbow – a colourful plate makes you feel great.

- Talk about food in terms of how it is grown, how it looks and tastes and feels. Involve children in cooking and cook from scratch as often as time allows.

- Answer with a question: do you enjoy this food? What do you think makes some foods more tasty than others? Do we all like the same things?

In closing, one important thing to consider in the middle of this is our own relationship with food and how that affects our kids.

But why aren't you eating chips, Mummy?

This question came from my own kids. Picture this: we were on holiday with friends and their kids in Salcombe, Devon. We'd been on a long walk (long in terms of time, not distance – there were three kids under four involved, so the pace was somewhere between a waddle and an amble). It was blustery and satisfying; we felt rosy-cheeked and invigorated as we bowled into a picturesque pub for lunch. And then, while the rest of the crew ordered fish and chips, I was so determined to be 'good', I ordered a salad.

To be clear, I love a good salad: they can be delicious and exciting. But we all know that there are places where salad is a token addition to the menu, where it will be a collection of stuff from the fridge rather than a nice culinary experience. And then there are places where they do excellent fish and chips, places where everyone in their right mind orders this. Not me. The food arrives. Everyone tucks into their delicious salty, carby, fatty confections, while I begin fiddling around with a limp salad leaf. At this point I had a realisation: it dawned on me that something was wrong. Eating healthily is good, but life is way too short not to enjoy fish and chips with people you love when by the sea.

What was I thinking in that Devon pub? It would have been fine for me not to eat those chips if I didn't fancy them. But as it was, it was an act of pure self-denial. Scarily, a teacher messaged me recently to say a seven-year-old in her class had said, 'I am trying not to eat carbs.' This was a wake-up moment. I want my kids to eat well and respect their bodies – and that means not getting sucked into the diet industry, which is worth a humongous $64 billion. An industry that to all intents and purposes is designed to make you fail.

Laura Thomas is clear that we should be aware of how important this is. 'The first thing I want to know about any parent who is concerned about their kid's nutrition is what is the parent's relationship with food. Are they relaxed about food and generally eat a wide variety and balance of foods; do they tend to overthink, micromanage and stress about food, or do they try to control their weight through restriction and avoiding foods? If it's the latter, it's worth looking at how we can improve our own relationship with food, as this becomes a blueprint for how our kids learn to relate to food and their bodies.'

The conversations I've had and the research I've conducted suggests this has the potential to be a significant issue. Of the 10,000 people I asked, 86 per cent had been on a diet, 23 per cent were currently on a diet, and 51 per cent intended to start the new year with a diet. AND, crucially, 87 per cent were conscious of passing food habits on to their kids.

So what steps can we take to improve our own relationship with food and prevent it becoming an issue with our kids?

- Don't talk about 'earning' food or 'regretting' food. Honour your hunger (and also your fullness).

- Speak kindly about yourself in relation to food.

- Be appreciative of the positive power of food beyond fuel.

- Food can be part of making memories and it's a tragedy to miss out on that. Eat mince pies at Christmas; enjoy really good bread and butter on a picnic; have a piece of cake on your kid's birthday. Screw the calories, enjoy the living.

- 'Never put kids on a diet!' says Laura passionately. 'Diets are harmful to kids. Their bodies are meant to grow, and kids will grow out before they grow up! Dieting is consistently shown to be one of the strongest predictors of eating disorders in children. They can also contribute towards negative body image and disordered eating (like overriding fullness signals or sneaking and stealing food). Girls gain an average of 13kg during adolescence (some will gain more!). Eating a balance and variety of foods and role modelling a healthy relationship with food are way better for kids than any restrictive diets.'

A more rounded and considered answer to the question of 'But why aren't you eating chips?' might be 'Because I don't fancy a whole plate of them now. I'd love to try one of yours – they look delicious!'

And in closing, a crucial point is this: nutrition doesn't need to be perfect, either in terms of what you are eating or what you are feeding you child.

Aim to be consistent and to offer the best you can – but cut yourself some slack. You can lead a kid to a balanced meal, but you cannot force them to eat. Laura Thomas says: 'Try to zoom out and look at the bigger picture – what are they eating over days, weeks and months rather than a single meal? Over time are they getting a variety of different foods from all food groups (and yes, carrots and cucumber sticks totally count!)? Also, even if their diet is relatively limited, take a step back and notice – are they growing well, sleeping okay, running around playing with loads of energy and doing well in school?'

She continues: 'Think about if they're hitting developmental milestones and doing well socially and emotionally – these things give us much greater insight into how a child is doing than whether or not they finished their peas!' I would add to that, think about how the mealtime feels, not what is eaten.

Don't focus on the carrot that was left on the side of the plate – instead talk about how delicious the pizza was, how nice it was to sit and chat, even if only for ten minutes.

That way you will be making happy food memories for your children.

BUT WHY DO PEOPLE
GET CANCER?

Why oh why? If only they didn't and if only this didn't need to be included in here. Cancer sucks. End of.

The real question here is how much is too much when it comes to talking to kids about cancer? Of course we don't want to burden them, but we also do want to normalise it.

Attempting to be frank and to avoid confusion, we told our kids that their granddad died because he was ill. In fact we came to realise that this wasn't completely frank and did lead to confusion. What followed was a barrage of questions, which resulted in our telling them he died of cancer.

There are a thousand new cancer cases in the UK every day. One in two people will get cancer in their lifetime. So there is a high chance it will impact a child's world. Which begs the question: how do we explain it to our kids?

I'm grateful to Cancer Research UK for the facts in this section and to high-profile members of the cancer community (they often joke it's the club nobody wants to be part of) to help answer this.

What is cancer?

Cancer Research UK has this explanation: 'Your body is made up of billions of tiny cells. Cells need to divide to replace ones that have worn out or become damaged. Normally they only divide when they need to, but sometimes this can go wrong and a cell keeps on dividing. When this happens, it is a cancer. There are lots of different types of cancer, depending on where in the body the first cell went wrong.'

The writer, speaker and columnist Emma Campbell was a single mum to triplets and their big brother when she was first diagnosed with breast cancer. She described it to her children like this: 'Cancer is when the cells in your body start growing too quickly and they clump together to make a lump which is called a tumour. It can be quite a nasty lump so the doctors give you really strong medicine to make it go away.'

From that, there are a few more things to consider: other questions that might follow, how and when to tell your kids when someone they know has it, wider thoughts that might help.

As far as other questions go, the most notable of interviewers really have nothing on a kid on a roll; there's nothing like an inquisitive five-year-old for firing off big question after big question. These are some you might come up against:

But why do people get it?

The facts are: we don't always know why people get cancer and it's often caused by things out of our control. Cancer Research UK suggests adding this nugget of truth: 'There are some things we can do to make it less likely, such as not smoking, eating healthily, exercising, and protecting our skin in the sun.'

Can children get cancer?

Gulp. Wouldn't it be nice to be able to answer a straight no here? I can't on the one hand call for truthfulness, and then hide from it when it gets uncomfortable. Instead, there is a way in that is honest but offers reassurance: 'Only a very small number of children get cancer. It is much more common in older people.'

How is it treated?

It can be treated in lots of different ways depending on the type of cancer. An operation to take the cancer out of the body is often helpful. There are also cancer-killing drugs called chemotherapy that can be used, as well as a special type of radiation.

From a personal point of view, Emma Campbell adds that the treatment can make you feel really poorly and look a bit funny as your hair can fall out. But the reason for that is that the treatment is strong and will eventually hopefully make you better.

It's a clever business. Doctors can now use drugs that target cancer cells and work with our immune system to get rid of the cancer too. New treatments are being discovered by scientists all the time, which is great news!

When will there be a cure for cancer?

'A lot of cancers can now be cured, especially if they are found early, and that includes many of the ones that children sometimes get. More people are being cured now than ever before and scientists are finding new treatments all the time, but there are still some cancers that are hard to treat,' say Cancer Research UK. Realistic and measured optimism is the tone on the wider conversation around cancer.

What if cancer affects your family directly?

Question is, what's the best approach when it's your family being impacted by cancer? Context is key. Not so long ago I recorded an episode of *Honestly* with two mates who are living with cancer. Deborah James has stage four cancer which is treatable but not curable. She has two children and chose not to tell them straight away. This is because with bowel cancer you don't know how advanced it is until you actually get the tumour out, so until she had that operation they didn't know how serious it was. She says: 'What I was hoping for is that I would never have to get to the whole "you've got advanced cancer" stage. They were seven and nine at the time, and they didn't need to know the word cancer. So we told them I was having an operation, but it was only then that we actually knew how serious it was.'

Bear in mind that kids' understanding may change during the course of your treatment. Especially if it spans a couple of years. A seven-year-old's comprehension may be very different from a five-year-old's. In this instance, your discussions should cater individually to each sibling and develop as they age. Discussions should also be led by their questions.

Two other great sources of information are Dr Liz O'Riordan, a consultant breast cancer surgeon, and Professor Trisha Greenhalgh, an academic and GP, who together authored *The Complete Guide to Breast Cancer*.[38] Both write from a particularly unique perspective: they are not only outstanding doctors, they have also experienced breast cancer first hand.

When talking about sharing the news with kids, they acknowledge that the 'how to do it' is often the hardest part, as it's a matter of pitching it right, depending on the age (and maturity) of the child.

The insights I took away from their book include:

- Though telling your kids may not be something you want to do, consider that kids have amazing intuition and will frequently pick up that something is going on.

- Remember that as their parent you are the expert on your children. You naturally know how best to talk to them. There is immense power in that. In fact, the doctors are quick to add that personal knowledge and relationships are every bit as important as any information they can give.

- Do some prep. Nothing too over the top, but figure out the language you might use to describe surgery or chemo. It's easier to have something prepared in your mind than to try to navigate it in the moment. Consider asking friends and family to use similar language for consistency.

- Some children find 'acting out' or 'drawing' their thoughts and questions easier than talking them through.

- Tell the school. That way they are prepped to offer support from their end.

- Keep disruption to family life as minimal as possible. That should be relatively possible with radiotherapy and surgery, say Greenhalgh and O'Riordan. However, chemotherapy is going to cause more upheaval. Ensure that the children know it is temporary and try to focus on some positives like getting more takeaways (because everyone is too weary to cook). If kids are off for sleepovers or playdates with other people, make sure that everyone helping out knows what exactly your child does or doesn't know. Avoid confusion!

Deborah James has this additional advice:

- Your relationships with pretty much everyone will change – some for the better, some for the worse.

- Just tell your kids how it is. They will worry less if they don't have to fill in the blanks themselves.

- Take the help. People are wonderful and want to help. Don't be embarrassed to be descriptive about the help you need.

- Be naughty, have lots of fun and blame the cancer!

- Love madly and deeply and kiss passionately.

- Make memories today to last a lifetime.

- Tell cancer to go fuck itself!

And remember, though nobody wants to find themselves talking about cancer with kids, be assured that kids are remarkably resilient when they have to be. This is something Audrey Allan, a.k.a. @cancerwithasmile, backed up in her Mother of All Lists post[39]; she was blown away by how quickly her kids accepted the news and the changes and were able to offer her support in the form of cuddles and giggles.

Also on that podcast with Debs James that I mentioned earlier was Saima Thompson, who was diagnosed with terminal cancer aged twenty-nine. As well as founding the ridiculously good Masala Wala Café, down the road from me in Brockley, Saima also set up a support group for BAME cancer sufferers. Devastatingly, she died in June 2020. Not only is my life better for having known Saima, but one bit of wisdom from that podcast will stay with me:

'My goal is ultimately to spend as much time with family and friends, pursue my passions and live life to the fullest. I want to show the world that a terminal diagnosis does not limit you to a "poor cancer patient" role.'

It's only in the face of death and illness that we are blessed with the ability to see what is really important. Of all the answers to all the questions, this is the lesson we truly want to land, isn't it?

BUT WHY DO ADULTS LIKE BEER AND WINE AND WHAT DOES IT EVEN DO?

So this is an interesting one to me. I gave up drinking in May 2019 after a very up-and-down relationship with it. When I tell people that, the next question is always an attempt to work out how much I drank and whether I had a 'problem'.

That's very hard to quantify. Alcohol wasn't going to cost me my relationship or my job. But alcohol was a terrible trigger for my mental health. It's normal for someone to know that caffeine doesn't agree with them: even one coffee might make them jittery. Even one drink made me anxious. There was also a huge level of shame involved. Hangovers were about feeling ashamed of what I had said, how I had behaved. And for a long time, I justified that in the name of fun.

Then the shame started showing her ugly, taunting face before I'd even gone out. I was caught between the public shame of not wanting to appear dull or boring by not drinking versus the inner shame that I wasn't listening to my instincts and honouring the fact that booze didn't work for me. Looking back at the (many) pictures of me drunk, I still feel that shame, but that's quickly followed by a massive sense of relief that the weight has been lifted. No regrets. No paranoia. No more excuses. No more shaming myself.

I have strong opinions about how drink culture in the UK is dangerous: you have a baby, you buy booze; get a promotion, toast your success with some fizz; go for a nice walk, stop at a pub. Flying somewhere? G&T on the plane. After work, because it's the weekend, because it's a big day . . . all are tied up with drinking. Something that is addictive and changes your rationale and inhibitions and significantly shifts your mood is not only available everywhere but it is encouraged.

So where does that leave me in relation to the question? I don't hate alcohol. I worry about the impact it has on so many lives and so many areas. I definitely don't want to pass on the shame to my kids.

But much like with sugar, demonising anything only risks making it into an appealing forbidden fruit. I hope my children have a balanced relationship with alcohol when they're older. Ben still drinks, as do most of my friends and family, and so, yet again, it's a case of modelling healthy consumption.

So why *do* some adults like alcohol?

Short answer: adults drink wine and beer for different reasons. When I put it out on Instagram, the replies were very much variations of the same thing: *'because it helps me relax . . . because I enjoy it . . . because it's fun! . . . because I like how it tastes'*. A few pointed out that it's something 'just for adults', while one brutally honest comment stood out to me: 'Not a clue. Thinking objectively, there's no good reason to drink other than it's fun sometimes.'

Longer answer: for this I looked to the team at Alcohol Change UK (alcoholchange.org.uk) and members of the sober community for help. The latter includes author Clare Pooley, whose book *The Sober Diaries*[40] is brilliantly frank about her relationship with booze, and Dave Wilson, a 'sobriety coach' (davidwilsoncoaching.com).

Your children might have questions about alcohol from an earlier age than you expected, say Alcohol Change UK.

Answer their questions honestly – be mindful. Often when we want to encourage children to drink in moderation we bring it to life with stories about our own drunk experiences, but we can end up making being drunk sound funny or exciting.

To avoid this, Clare and Dave suggest introducing the subject of hangovers as a nod to the negatives. Clare went with: 'Getting drunk is when grown-ups drink too much alcohol because they think it'll make them have more fun or feel more relaxed, but it actually makes them do stupid things and feel really sick the next day.'

Dave added: 'Being drunk is what happens when you don't just have one or two glasses of wine or beer. Drinking too much can make you feel a bit strange and act really silly. Sometimes we make decisions we wouldn't normally make. Some people feel very sleepy when they drink too much and wake up the next day with a terrible headache.'

But what about the broader picture? Of the 2,000 people I asked, 87 per cent drank alcohol and the large majority did so in front of their kids, while only 38 per cent admitted they had been 'drunk' in front of them.

On further enquiry on how they felt about being drunk around their kids, opinions seemed to be vehemently divided. Half felt absolutely fine or ambivalent, while others expressed guilt, embarrassment, shame, regret, even fear at 'what could have happened while I was out of control'.

Several people fell into a camp of 'defiantly okay', confident in their choice because in their minds either their kids hadn't noticed or had found it funny. Or just that it wasn't even an issue. Some felt it was actively positive: '*It normalised alcohol for them . . . It's good for them to see an example that isn't binge drinking . . . I'm a happy drunk so it's not a problem.*'

It seems 'how drunk' is the key thing for many. Certain phrases came up: '*just merry . . . not drunk drunk . . . not obliterated . . . never wasted; I would never want to be out of control in front of my kids . . . I don't get drunk in front of them, but they have seen me have a glass of wine.'*

Though, to be a bit of a bore for a moment, if you remember from when you were pregnant, people who are drinking are not necessarily the best at gauging their own drunkenness, are they?! Or maybe that was just me.

Other perspectives were very much informed by their parents: *'My father was a terrible drunk so I'm very careful . . . My parents got drunk in front of us growing up and it's not something I want to repeat for my children . . . My mum used to drink around me and I hated it, so I never want my son to see that.'* Or at the opposite end of the scale: *'My mum despised alcohol because both her parents were alcoholics. As a result, I grew up excessively fearful of alcohol, and I don't want my kids to feel as extreme as that . . . My parents never drank; if I saw it more openly in a social setting maybe I'd have binged less.'*

Some had ideas around specific boundaries. One person said they drank *'only when there is a sober adult present'*. Others were passionate about *'showing you can enjoy alcohol responsibly . . . Normalising it takes away the excitement'*. And some people felt equally strongly against it: *'Teetotal by choice. Can't drink and parent, simple as that . . . For me, being drunk is a no go. I want my daughter to grow up feeling she is always safe with me.'*

I have to say I was surprised by the spectrum of answers, not from a place of judgement, but more that it seems it's one of those topics where people have specific and often very personal views on what's appropriate and what's not.

Digging a bit further, I asked Instagram: 'what do you wish you had known about booze when you were younger?' Answers included:

- That drinking doesn't have to mean getting drunk.

- That you don't need it to have fun.

- That it never helps a bad day or situation.

- Too much is never a good thing.

- That nothing good comes of it.

- What hangovers are and how ill they can make you feel.

- That it is addictive. Really addictive.

- That it affects different people in different ways.

- That it can make you make strange choices and do things you might regret.

- That you don't have to be drinking in the morning to have a problem.

- That drunk doesn't makes things better, it makes things different and that parties and weddings are just as fun without.

Why not gently bring some of these things into the conversation if your kids ask you about alcohol? Being honest in this way also backs up the advice from Alcohol Change UK, who have seen that frank chat with kids from when they're little lays the groundwork for an open relationship when they're older – and evidence shows that this is one of the most important factors in developing healthy drinking habits. As they enter their teens, encourage your kids to talk to you about where they're going when they go out, what sort of things they get up to, and who their friends are. That way you can spot any problems and help your children to resolve them.

The truth is, though, that kids learn more from what they see you do than what they hear you say, so my best advice is to try to only drink alcohol in front of them when it's a special occasion. Don't let it become part of their everyday memories or let them see you drinking alone, or they'll think that's normal. Show them how to drink responsibly, and hopefully they will too.

How to help your kids grow up with a healthy relationship with alcohol:

Many of us probably don't think all that much about alcohol and our kids – at least not until they're teenagers. But children *do* think about alcohol from a surprisingly young age. And evidence shows that there are some things we as parents can do to help them grow up to have a healthy, happy relationship with alcohol.

Alcohol Change UK give this advice: 'If your children see that you seem to need alcohol to socialise, relax or de-stress, you might be sending out messages you don't want them to pick up. That doesn't mean that you have to be teetotal, but setting an example that you'd like your children to follow is a good general guide.'

Inevitably, that might mean asking yourself some tricky questions about your own drinking. So, what should you do if you think you are drinking too much?

According to data released by Google, searches for 'Am I an alcoholic?' or some variant of that went up 1,700 per cent in 2020.

What a statistic. My empathy is with the people who are in that place and also for the kids involved. Though it might not be what we want to hear, Alcohol Change UK say: 'Children tend to notice when their parents are drinking frequently or heavily, even if they're quite young. This can be scary for them, and can mean that they have practical or emotional needs that aren't being met.'

Of course, this is all on a sliding scale. Not surprisingly, I would advocate for the benefits of sobriety here. There's nothing quite like the joy of waking up with a clear head and being able to remember every moment of the day before with clarity. However, I do know that route isn't for everyone, or it can be something you come to only over time.

That said, even just cutting back on your alcohol intake can have big benefits for you as well as for your kids. Simple ways to do this, as suggested by Alcohol Change UK, include:

- Keeping track of how much you're drinking. You could use an app to help you.

- Setting goals for cutting back, for example some days off each week, or limiting your drinking to a certain number of units.

- Thinking about how much alcohol you keep in the house – if you've got it in the cupboard or the fridge, it's all too easy to drink it.

- Getting some extra support if you need it. You can speak to your GP or local alcohol service (find yours on the NHS website) and get help that's right for you.

So how *can* we help our kids have a healthy relationship with alcohol? That's the million-dollar question and there is no sure-fire solution, but research suggests that there are two things parents can do to improve the chances of this happening: be open and honest, and set clear, firm and fair boundaries when it comes to drinking.

Incidentally, some popular wisdom suggests we should adopt a 'Continental' approach and give our children small amounts of alcohol to help them learn to drink sensibly. It's certainly an idea I have heard bandied around, but even as I type it, it feels a bit bonkers. As does the historic law that states any child aged five or older can have an alcoholic drink at home or in any private house! Madness.

Alcohol Change UK are adamant that there's very little evidence that the Continental approach works. In fact: 'Research shows that the younger a person is when they first get drunk, the more at risk they are of developing alcohol problems later in life.' The UK's chief medical officers say that children shouldn't drink at all until at least fifteen years old, and even after this only very small amounts, and no more than once a week. The main reason for this is that young people's bodies and brains are continuing to grow and change, so alcohol can cause serious and long-lasting damage, including memory problems and difficulty learning.

And if that wasn't compelling enough, it seems often the idea to give alcohol to minors comes from the parents, not the children. In fact, more and more young people are drinking less or not at all. As that trend continues, it might be that more parents will be challenged by their children about their drinking!

Remember that you are still important to your children even when they are teenagers. Parents often underestimate how much influence they have on older children, especially when it comes to alcohol – but what you say and do can make a real difference. The truth is that helping young people have a healthy relationship with alcohol doesn't always have much to do with alcohol itself. Self-confidence and a sense of self-worth are what matters most. That comes down to things you're probably already doing: spending time with them, being ready to listen, and making clear rules and sticking to them.

Wahhhh! I can't even imagine actual teenagers. While I hope that by then I won't be worrying so much about how much pesto pasta they eat or having to persuade them to put their shoes on, there is a whole world to navigate in terms of new, uncharted waters. In some ways it will be a case of crossing that bridge when we come to it, but there's definitely a benefit to laying foundations for clear communication at a young age, even about subjects that might seem grown-up. Start the conversation about booze young, but definitely don't encourage consumption until they are much older.

When I started looking for answers to the questions raised in this section, I had hoped to keep my response neutral, even though alcohol consumption is something I feel strongly about. Then during the research process I received an email that really hit a nerve.

It was from Dr Eleanor Ryan-Saha, a research volunteer for NACOA (the National Association for Children of Alcoholics). She wrote a powerful piece for Mother of All Lists on being a Child of an Alcoholic (COA).[41] I'd recommend reading the whole thing, but here is an extract:

- I think with an alcoholic parent it's the lying that's the worst. You are brought up to trust them implicitly. That betrayal is what you never get over.

- My mum's alcoholism destroyed our family in a sort of slow-motion car crash way, but no one could really wade in and help . . . we were otherwise a very unexceptional British family. I've seen how alcoholism is one of the most pervasive aspects of our modern lives in the UK.

- It's impossible as a COA to have an easy relationship with drinking. We rarely have alcohol in the house because I find bottles of alcohol in a home environment, especially spirits, really unnerving. I want to model an easy, responsible relationship with alcohol to my children when they are older, so I will have a glass of wine in front of them, but no more. I'm struggling to balance making them feel comfortable and staying comfortable myself.

- There is so, so much work to be done in the UK when it comes to alcoholism and parenthood. I feel strongly that the 'wine o'clock' and 'adult headache' aspect of motherhood is one of the most damaging exclusionary discourses, and little to nothing is being said about it. Alcohol is many things to many people, but never is it self-care. However, I wonder if this might be one of the most unpopular positions you could take in the UK. I've often noticed that if you want to make conversation, you comment on the weather, but if you want to make a friend, you joke about alcohol. Reacting negatively to depictions of drinking makes you a killjoy.

- Behind every alcoholic parent, there is a child of an alcoholic. I always say I can see a reason for addiction, but never an excuse. I love my mum, and it's not her fault. But there is no excuse for bringing children into the world, only to subject them to alcoholism. Would it be so hard for parents to have a really big think about their relationship with alcohol? Or the way they talk about alcohol to other adults and to children? Is it really a 'buzz kill' to ask that we no longer promote alcohol as desirable or find alcoholism funny?

These are uncomfortable questions to end on, but they are important to sit with, especially in relation to how we want the next generation to cultivate a relationship with booze.

BUT WHY DO I HAVE TO
SAY SORRY?

Knee-jerk answer: BECAUSE I ASKED YOU TO! (This is particularly intense when your child has done something awful to another kid.) However, on reflection, 'sorry' is very nuanced.

In his piece for *Psychology Today*, Dr Fredric Neuman walks us through why demanding an apology might be best avoided, saying we should never apologise just to make peace or if we don't genuinely feel contrite.[42] Although set against that, of course, saying sorry when we do something wrong, or when we are not 'good', is the honourable thing to do. It acknowledges that your choices have negatively affected others.

Esther Perel, a therapist and author, said recently on the TED podcast, *WorkLife*[43]: 'The acknowledgement involves an element of remorse or guilt – sometimes for what you've done to the other person, not necessarily for your own action.'

A 'sorry' used too liberally, though, can be problematic.

In an article for the *New York Times*, social scientist Adam Grant explains that as early as age five or six, children spontaneously say they're sorry for hurting their peers, and even occasionally their siblings.[44] As parents it's good that we have instilled that reflex in our kids, but it's bad if they don't join the dots of how and why. You see, as Neuman says, that willingness to apologise is actually a willingness to step up and shoulder responsibility. It's one thing suggesting a child 'should say sorry', it's another helping them to realise that they 'want to make amends'. The value of an apology is in the feelings attached to it.

In child counselling (particularly trauma-informed), rather than forcing a child to say sorry there is an emphasis on 'finding opportunities to repair'. So rather than Hannah having to apologise to Holly for knocking over her tower, you would encourage her to see the issue, e.g. 'Poor Holly, she has been working hard on that tower, and now she seems upset', followed by, 'I wonder what we could do to make her feel better?'

The thought being that by taking this approach, the repair is in a decisive, meaningful action, not in a word said under duress.

Also take a moment to consider when, as adults, we use sorry in the wrong places. You don't need to say you're sorry when you say no to something you can't or don't want to do. It's not wrong. It's just the way it is. So don't insert 'sorry' in the place of 'no thank you'.

Delete unnecessary apologies in work emails. You are not sorry you can't make the 6.30 p.m. meeting because you have to look after your child. You haven't done anything wrong or inflicted harm on anyone else (as per the definition of an apology). So instead simply go for 'I can't make the 6.30 p.m. meeting.'

Don't say sorry because you ask a (potentially) valid question. There's no such thing as a stupid question. Often, in a group situation, other people are thinking it too and are glad you are the one who piped up.

Don't say sorry because you think you should. Or because you have been pressurised into it. An insincere apology is worse than saying nothing. A performative sorry is even worse.

Do check your tone and eye contact. If someone deserves a sorry from you, the least you can do is to say it properly, even if it is uncomfortable.

Do say sorry when something bad has happened to someone (a death or illness or break-up). But fight the urge to then minimise it: avoid saying 'he had a good innings', 'maybe it was meant to be', or 'you'll get another job easily'. All that serves to do is make the tricky situation easier for you as the 'apologiser' but actually detracts from the sincerity and simplicity of an expression of empathy.

I have also taught my kids to follow up a 'sorry' with: 'Are you okay?' or 'Would you like to talk about it?' or 'Is there anything I can do to help?'

In my experience, it's worth being picky when you use a 'sorry'. Stop throwing them around and making them worthless. Save them up, then they really are something valuable and potentially powerful too. If your kids see you do this, it will come naturally to them too.

JOINING BIT SIX:

LISTEN TO YOUR TRUTH

The greatest burden a child must bear is the unlived life of its parents.[45]

Carl Jung

Time and time again during this process – of writing and of raising kids – I've been struck by the realisation that while I am busy trying to teach them stuff, they are actually the ones teaching me.

One day I found myself laughing in awe at Greta. In the space of an hour she showed me that she was already what I wanted to be. There were tunes playing downstairs on Spotify and she bowled in from nowhere, naked apart from wings and a pair of her brother's pants, and yelled: 'Come on, Mummy, dance with me!' So I did.

Earlier that day, she'd banged her head on the corner of the table. Standard toddler accident. Bursting into tears, she simply said, 'I need a hug.' Of course we all obliged.

And then lastly, as Ben piled the three of them into the car to go to his mum's, she gave me a kiss and said, 'Bye, Mummy, you'll really miss me.' She was spot on: I did. That's a girl who knows her worth, who can express her needs in an unapologetic way. To use an American expression, she is 'living her truth'.

So how do I ensure that she stays that way? The answer is, yet again, by modelling it myself: by being okay with my own truth.

As they pulled away that day in the car (leaving me to stay and work on this book), I was overwhelmed with guilt. I felt guilty that I wouldn't see them for a couple of days but what I felt REALLY guilty about was wanting space on my own.

I had to talk myself through it.

If I want Greta to continue to be as sure of herself as she is, to be able to express her needs, then I need to show that in myself. I shouldn't feel I have to apologise for some alone time, at any time, but ESPECIALLY off the back of lockdown, when we had literally been together non-stop for months.

I was blown away by Glennon Doyle's book *Untamed*,[46] which is page after page of insight, a real invitation to live an empowered version of your life. When Glennon urges us to be untamed, she is asking us to be who we truly are. To go for what we want. Offering yourself freedom is a gift for your kids.

I often hold in my head an idea of what it is to be a good mother, wife, daughter, friend, sister or person to work with. But I rarely, or not until recently, check in with what it means to be the me I truly want to be.

Listen to your own truth! Tune out the parent guilt and allow space to 'be in touch with who you are'.

Your reaction to that might be: 'I know who I am.' And if you do, then that is amazing.

My experience of that is different: firstly I feel like I am constantly becoming a different version of myself. But also, in the throes of motherhood, I lost myself. It was a combination of self-deprivation and the fact that having a baby changes your body, your finances, your career, your relationship, your friendships, your freedom, your independence, your rest and your fun.

While trying to figure out how to navigate all of that, it can be hard to remember or discover who you are. One day I was thirty and pregnant: blink and I am approaching thirty-nine, and at times I feel more like Bertie, Woody and Greta's mum than I do Clemmie. It's not that I don't want to give them everything they need, it's that I also need to do that by supporting 'me' as well.

There are other issues at play here too, and they are the distraction of other people's voices and the pursuit of validation from others, both of which have been amplified by social media.

Glennon says that in order to be true to ourselves, we have to rediscover and be guided by our own inner voice.

In celebration of intuition:

The word intuition comes from the word *intuir*, meaning 'knowledge from within'. Intuition promises that if we look within ourselves, we can access depths that are simply off limits in the concrete, external world of facts and figures. This is not new or new-fangled. Albert Einstein said, 'Intuition, not intellect, is the "open sesame" of yourself.'

Intuition is really power. Proof of that can be seen in a study conducted by cognitive psychologist Gary Klein, in which he studied how firefighters make decisions in the workplace. He was surprised to discover that firefighters claimed that they didn't 'make decisions' at all, in so far as they didn't actively choose between any options. They simply acted and reacted based on their previous experiences without trying to come up with different courses of action.

As parents, this is something we have innately too. We learn to know when our sick kid has gone from being not quite right to something to be worried about. Beauty guru Caroline Hirons claims that she could smell when her four kids were under the weather. It's weird, but I think I know what she means.

If something feels off, it more than likely is. Gut feelings are real feelings.

Yet we are quick to look for answers elsewhere rather than trusting our own instincts. This habit is not exclusive to women but it's prevalent amongst them. In *Untamed*, Glennon Doyle tells a story of asking a bunch of kids (her daughter and her friends) if they were hungry and wanted something to eat. The boys said yes without thinking. The girls looked at one another, then one girl spoke on behalf of them all saying, 'No, we're fine.'

Believe me, I get the irony of this. This whole book is me attempting to answer questions via asking for loads of other people's opinions. And I stand by that notion because I want to check in with other experiences.

However, there is a difference between seeking insight in order to better inform ourselves (which is good) and only looking for outside opinion because we don't have the confidence to trust our own intuition.

How can we better access our intuition?

There are times when my intuition or gut feeling has sorted me right out. Even down to not going to something for no other reason than it didn't 'seem right'. Or when you text someone just because you felt they could do with a check-in and they reply with gratitude. It sounds crackers, but in those moments, do acknowledge where your intuition came good. An awareness of that gut feeling is the first step to harnessing its power.

Part of tuning in to our inner sense involves tuning out the outer voices where possible (which goes back to the invitation to 'find silence').

Feeling a bit wobbly doesn't mean you are wrong. Feeling wobbly about having the confidence of one's convictions is partly because we are simply out of practice. Try not to default to Google or other people's advice. Instead, like a muscle, the more we flex our intuition the more stable it becomes.

The wobble also comes because listening to our truth and following our inner voice also means taking responsibility.

I counter that feeling with the knowledge that if you don't like how things turn out, there's the opportunity to choose differently the next time.

In every situation there are countless alternatives that affect you and those around you, but a mistake learned from following your gut is a thousand times easier to live with than one that feels forced upon you because you went with someone else's version of the truth. To put it another way, a decision that goes against your gut is a mistake. Whereas one that goes with it can't really go wrong, it's just an opportunity for learning.

How does this relate to your kids' questions?

Your intuitive response to a question is powerful. Of course, back that answer up with research, with hard and fast information and science, and perhaps some of the perspectives shared in here.

But that nudge from your soul (which incidentally is very different from the knee-jerk reaction to keep them quiet and hope they'll go to sleep) – that intuition is the one to listen to. It's based on knowing the kid in front of you in a way that only a parent can, and viewing the issue through the lens of your own unique experiences.

Let's face it, there is no map. No one else has stood there with your child and each of their individual needs and experiences. Every life is an experiment.

We can't teach our kids if we aren't willing to learn, but also kids don't want us to be flawless and finite. And they are more likely to trust us if we trust ourselves.

We want them to ask *and* answer the questions. To be the truest version of themselves (or indeed to stay closer to the wonderful person they already are, the one that is broadly untainted by the outside world). Then we need to do our best to be that person too.

When I was a kid, I wish I had known that . . . I already had the perfect life; it was one without worry or stress and every day I woke up only thinking of that one. Too many people spend their lives sacrificing their health to gain money, when at the end of their lives they would give every penny back to regain their health, live a simple life, see the world and make many people smile along the way.

Ben Tansley @tano_hg

7

THE BIG QUESTIONS

Here we go. The final push. Throughout this journey of self-discovery (a.k.a. questioning everything I thought I knew about everything, ever), I hope that I have learned a bit about how to approach the questions, regardless of the actual subject. And, better still, I hope that I have gone some way towards sharing that with you.

With that in mind it would be great to cruise easily towards the end. Sadly, that isn't the case. I decided to go out with a bang. The final push, as it were; by that I mean a bunch of whopping great questions that quite frankly I'd prefer to bypass altogether rather than face. Unfortunately, given the size and weight of them, they aren't easily swept under the carpet . . . so let's get cracking.

BUT HOW DO BABIES GET IN MUMMIES' TUMMIES?

It's the sex question. It's the sex question. It's the sex question. Like a siren in my mind. Except for it's not. The only panic around this is the fact that it's just so blooming abstract, isn't it?

After a quick perusal of parenting forums there seems to be a variety of answers to this. And some of them, in my opinion, are pretty weird. There was talk of 'mixing ingredients like a cake and then it grows in your tummy oven'. I usually love any kind of food analogy but that made me want to vom. Cake and semen should never be mixed. Even metaphorically.

Some mentioned 'fairy dust' and 'baby dancing'; others talk of a 'special cuddle'. Frankly, saying the words 'special cuddle' also triggers my gag reflex, especially since the reality is generally a perfunctory well-timed bonk.

Other answers included 'babies come from a twinkle in Daddy's eye'. BULLSHIT. 'Daddy picked the brightest star in the sky and Mummy ate it.' Enough about Daddy already. Although one woman messaged me to say that the actual reason Mummy had a baby in her tummy was 'Daddy didn't pull out quickly enough!' Classic Daddy.

I was surprised to read that some people told their kids that it was down to Jesus. Now, I am not challenging anyone's religious beliefs but I am fairly sure that isn't what the Bible teaches. Are we trying to have the next generation believe that JC impregnates every woman on Earth (think Father Christmas but much more worn out)? Again, it's not my place to judge. But I do know that while I want to leave lots of room for discovery/exploration for my kids, I feel it is our responsibility to equip them with the truth, a.k.a. the biological facts.

The most common route to conception is this – a daddy puts his penis in the mummy's vagina, sperm comes out and finds the egg inside the mummy's womb. This isn't the tummy – it's something underneath your tummy. When the egg and the sperm meet they do something called 'fertilise'.

This is factually and biologically accurate. Use the words 'uterus/womb', not 'tummy'. Use the word 'sex' too (but prepare for more questions).

Things to consider 1) Babies don't always make it into wombs in the same way

Speaking to parents in the IVF, surrogacy and donor community, there is mixed opinion on how vital it is to say that conception doesn't always happen naturally.

Liv Throne had her son Herb via a sperm donor. He is only two now and she has yet to answer the 'baby in mummy's tummy' question, but there is an air of despondency from her as she talks about the friction from the community on how best to do it. She feels strongly that nobody gets to police anyone for their choices. The bottom line for her is it's her child and she plans to be straightforward: 'I'm going to tell him the facts and tailor the language based on age. We have been really honest with my adopted niece and nephew – no pandering or babyish language. I plan to say things like: "You need an egg and a seed. I had an egg, but needed a seed. A man gave his seed and a doctor put it into my tummy to make it grow into a baby." Specifically HIM. Crucially, he will know there was a doctor involved, that it was clinical.'

Things to consider 2) Sometimes it works, sometimes it doesn't

When discussing conception with your child, consider whether to acknowledge that sometimes making a baby doesn't 'just happen'.

According to Clearblue (the people who make pregnancy tests), only a third of couples conceive in the first month. If you're under thirty-five it's normal for it to take up to a year and 67 per cent will get pregnant within the first two years. I am not suggesting that you bombard your kid with the data, but there could be something to be said for setting out the reality that conception can take time.

Things to consider 3) Where is the line between physical and emotional?

Framing things scientifically can often feel like the right option when it comes to explaining conception, but do bear in mind how you want to reference the emotional side of it too. You might want to mention that making a baby is an act of love: in many instances between the couple, but if you're talking about IVF/surrogacy it can extend further.

Even clinical processes are human interactions. It's something Liv feels very strongly about; speaking as if to Herb, she says: 'It's what Mummy really wanted: *you* were really wanted, so the doctor helped Mummy,' and 'The doctor and the man gave Mummy the seed to help Mummy because she wanted to love you.'

Other things to mention:

- There are mummies and mummies and daddies and daddies too.

- Some people choose to have babies on their own.

- Some people's babies are grown in other people's tummies before they become adopted by the daddies or mummies.

- Not everyone can have babies.

- Not everyone wants to have babies.

In other words, this question is not just an opportunity to talk about how people get pregnant, it's also a chance to normalise other types of families.

How to pitch it?

This was something that worried me. Interestingly, I discovered that the kids found their own level with it.

At seven, Bertie's asked a lot more questions (including whether it hurts when the willy goes in the vagina!), whereas five-year-old Woody was interested in the broad notion of it, then lost interest and went back to whatever game he was playing.

Sex therapist and sexual health nurse Cath Hakanson says this is normal: 'If they don't understand what you have said, they'll promptly forget whatever it is. Don't stress about saying too much! Luckily for us parents, kids have inbuilt safety switches and promptly forget anything that they don't understand. So you don't have to worry about sparking their curiosity about stuff that they just aren't ready for!' Great advice!

Once I got past the awkwardness of the subject with my kids, they were soon preoccupied with the miracle of the fact that they were once actually inside me. I talked about feeling them squirm and hiccup and that it was tiring but that I loved it. I have their scan photos on the bedroom wall and I enjoyed showing them those too.

I opened this question by saying it's THE SEX QUESTION, but it's not really. It's the conception question!

A bit on sex education:

Cath Hakanson reminded me that kids start noticing pregnancy and babies when they're around three to four years of age. To satisfy their curiosity they'll begin to ask questions about babies – they are trying to understand why they are here, why they exist. The earlier you start talking to your kids about this stuff, the simpler the answers need to be and the better versed you'll be by the time you get to the really 'sticky' (bleurgh) sex stuff.

Hakanson also made a very important point that is applicable to much of this book. 'You want to be their main source for information. And for some strange reason, answering questions like "Where do babies come from?" lets kids know that you're okay with talking about that stuff because, as your child grows older, they will be exposed to sexual information that you have no control over. So you want them to know that if they hear anything that they don't understand, *you* are the person to come to. Not their friends, and definitely not Google. This way you can make sure that your child receives the right information and you can correct any misinformation that they hear.'

As such she advises being matter-of-fact. React as if the question is no more loaded than them asking how cereal gets in a bowl.

Another great tool is asking what they think. That way you can work out what they already know and what they actually want to know. Make sure that you give them enough information so that they don't make wrong conclusions. And, luckily for you, kids usually only want one snippet of information at a time. So, a three-year-old may want to know where babies come from but usually won't want to know how the baby got inside. How they understand things just isn't advanced enough for that type of information yet. And remember every child is different. Some kids may not be curious about where babies come from until they are four or five or even older. Some kids never ask!

Hakanson also pulled together this brilliantly comprehensive guide to what you can talk about with your children and when, which I have borrowed with her permission:

✳ Early childhood (two to five years): ✳

Our bodies

- Teach children the correct names of the body parts and what they do.

- Boys and girls are different but are also the same – girls usually have a vulva, boys usually have a penis but we all have nipples/bottoms/noses/hands, etc.

- Our bodies are different and that is okay to be different.

Privacy

- Some parts of the body are private – these aren't for the whole world to see.

- There are private and public places and times – this one is a tricky one for kids to learn, because it does tend to change. For example, it might be okay for your child to be naked at home when Granny is visiting, but not when the plumber is there!

- They need to learn to respect other people's privacy. For example, if the bathroom door is closed, they should knock and ask if they can come in.
- They are entitled to privacy too if they want it – like when they go to the toilet, are in the bath or getting dressed.

Touching ourselves

- It is okay to touch their penis or vulva. Explain that touching your own genitals can feel good but it should happen in a private place, like in their bedroom!
- If your child grabs their genitals when they are out socially, gently remind them that they need to keep their hands out of their pants. Don't make a big fuss as they are doing it because it makes them feel more secure. Don't worry – they will grow out of it! (Hope so!)

Babies

- Tell them that all living things reproduce – trees drop seeds, dogs have puppies and humans have babies. Slowly start pointing out examples of reproduction when you see them.
- How a baby is made – that you need a part from a man (cell or sperm) and a part from a woman (cell or egg) to make a baby.
- A baby grows inside a woman; in their uterus.
- If they want to know how the baby comes out, just explain that it comes out of the woman's stomach or through her vagina.
- Making babies is for adults and not something kids do. (It's good to get into reminding them of this regularly, perhaps even every time you talk about it.)

Body ownership and touching

- They are the boss of their body and have a right to say who can touch their body (you included).

- It is not okay to hug or touch someone if they don't want you to (and vice versa).

- Sometimes there are reasons for an adult to look at or touch their body, like a doctor or nurse.

- We don't keep secrets about our bodies. They can always tell you about anything that makes them feel bad or funny.

Middle childhood (five to eight years):

Our bodies

- Know what words to use when talking about body parts (both boys and girls) – penis, testicles, scrotum, anus, vulva, labia, vagina, clitoris, uterus and ovaries.

- Give them some knowledge of the internal reproductive organs – uterus, ovaries, fallopian tubes, urethra, bladder, bowel.

- Bodies come in all different shapes, sizes and colours.

- Teach them to be able to look after their own body, i.e. private parts, hair, teeth, skin, etc.

- Teach them to have refusal skills in place – 'Stop, I don't like that.'

Sexual intercourse

- A baby can happen when a man's sperm joins a woman's ovum and it usually happens by sexual intercourse (IVF is another way).

- A baby is made when sperm leave the man through his penis and go into the woman's vagina. They then find their way to the place where the egg is. The egg and the sperm then join together, and grow into a baby.

- Adults have sex and it's a natural, normal and healthy part of life.

- Sex is an adult activity and is not for kids.

- Adults can choose whether or not to have a baby.

Sexual behaviour

- Masturbation – some kids do and some don't.

- All sexual behaviour is private, i.e. masturbation, sexual intercourse.

- Bodies can feel good when touched.

- Sometimes people look at pictures of naked people or people having sex on the internet and this is not for kids. You also need to discuss with your child what they should do when (not if) they come across these images.

- Explain that there are different sexual orientations such as heterosexual, homosexual, and bisexual.

✳ **Later childhood (eight to thirteen years):** ✳

Puberty

- Teach them all of the above but in much greater detail.

- Remind them what physical, social and emotional changes to expect with puberty (both sexes).

- Girls need to know to be prepared for their first period.

- Boys need to know about ejaculation and wet dreams.

- Fertility happens once girls start having periods and boys start producing semen.

- Both boys and girls are able to make babies after they have reached puberty.

Sexual behaviour

- Some kids are curious about sex and some aren't. Both are normal. Once puberty starts, they will slowly start to think about sex as being something that they may someday want to do. By starting conversations about sex with your child, you are letting them know that it is okay for them to come to you with any questions.

- Gradually give them more details about sexual intercourse and other sexual behaviours.

- Give basic information about STIs (Sexually Transmitted Infections) as they may hear about them – sometimes you can catch infections when you have sexual intercourse but there are ways to make sex safer.

- Give basic information about how to avoid pregnancy – there are things you can do to prevent it.

- Foster awareness of their parents' sexual values and beliefs – love, dating, contraception, when it is okay to become sexually active, etc.

- Once puberty starts, they will slowly start to feel more sexual and develop romantic feelings towards their peers.

- Once puberty starts, same-sex fantasy and attraction is not unusual and does not necessarily indicate sexual orientation.

- Sexuality is exaggerated in pornography.

- Teach them how to be cybersmart and to use their mobile phone safely.

- Teach them the characteristics of respectful relationships.

For this section I also consulted clinical sexologist Georgia Rose, who wrote a brilliant piece for Mother of All Lists on how to talk to your kids about sex.[47] It's frank and informative and well worth reading in full. She talks about how good sex ed is not happening in schools, and how most kids learn about sex through speaking with friends (often inaccurate), media representations of sex scenes (unrealistic) and, worst of all, porn (you don't need me to explain why this is disastrous). This leaves us parents to do the heavy lifting. She reminds us that – although it brings its own problems – the internet can also be a helpful source of information. And she is an advocate of lifelong learning on the subject, for us as well as for our kids.

'As we grow and change, and get to know ourselves better with age,' she says, 'we deserve to devote time and energy into our sexual schooling and sexual wellness. This is especially critical since so many of us had such lacklustre sex education at school – we have a lot of holes to fill (pun intended!) and time to make up!'

When I was a kid, I wish I had known that . . .
sex education extends further than condoms
and bananas and chlamydia. The hush around
sexual violence and misogyny left me and my
peers more vulnerable entering the world as
young women.

Erin Smithers @noandroblog

BUT WHY IS YOUR TUMMY
SO SQUISHY, MUMMY?

Working as a counterpoint to the 'why is her tummy so big?' question that many kids ask on seeing a pregnant woman, are these 'classic' ones aimed at us mothers, which are likely to be familiar to many of us, particularly postpartum:

'Are you pregnant, Mummy?' (I gave birth six years ago.) 'Look at Mummy with her really big wobbly belly!' Or: 'Your tummy is exactly like playdough!' Or the equally charming: 'Why does your belly point down?'

Short answer: is it? Thank you! All the better for you to cuddle it.

Long answer: let's meet that question in the spirit it was intended: out of curiosity. And probably with a big, deep breath. Someone told me that your first reaction to something is what you have been taught, the second reaction is what you've learned. I am okay with questions like this, but it takes a moment to get there.

Here are the, perhaps obvious, steps I go through. A tummy is just a tummy, in the same way a hand is just a hand. It is only because of the value we affix to it that these words pack such a punch. The media have flogged the belief that if we simply commit to glugging skinny tea (a.k.a. shit-yourself tea) or take a 'six weeks to a six-pack challenge' then we too could have abs of steel. They make it sound so easy, but here's the catch: it's actually set up to ensure you're guaranteed to lose. Clever, huh?

During a counselling session with the London Centre for Intuitive Eating, who specialise in non-diet approaches to nutrition, I remember a particularly revealing conversation that went like this:

> Me: I'd love to try what it's like to have a six-pack for a day.
>
> Counsellor: Why? What would you do with it?
>
> Me: Errr . . . I'd take my top off a lot. And I'd wear a lot of crop tops.
>
> Counsellor: And then what? Beyond the crop tops, how else would the flat tummy enhance your life?
>
> Me: Um . . .

I was flummoxed. The truth is, having a six-pack wouldn't make the slightest bit of difference to anything. It wouldn't make me more successful. It wouldn't make me more loved. It wouldn't make me a better or kinder person. And yet I had fixated on it my entire life! Hours and hours spent punishing myself to try to achieve it. What a wally.

The answer was quite literally staring me in the face. My squishy tummy was the result of my best achievement: growing my three favourite humans.

It sounds pukey but it's true. My kids are better than a washboard stomach any day. But even if the tummy wasn't a tummy and it didn't grow humans (don't write in; as I've talked about earlier, I do know it's a womb that grows the baby), even if it was something less significant like an earlobe or a philtrum or the third toe on your left foot, the human body is amazing.

Next time you are reacting to a potentially negative-feeling comment about yourself: stop (i.e. don't go with any immediate gut reaction). As per the above, have a word with yourself; how would having the 'ideal' version of that body part you have in mind really make a difference to your life? Then look at that body part on a child. Look how perfect it is. Your version of whatever it is – upper arm, thigh, left boob, whatever – really is just as amazing.

And while six-packs have a certain appeal, the fact that my body once rearranged its organs to bring another life into the world means this wobbly tummy is some kind of wonderful.

When I was a kid, I wish I had known that . . .
what Grandma told me about weight being
really important was in fact complete nonsense
and merely a reflection of her reality . . . and
that being gay and a bit weird was completely
okay.

Jules Von Hep @julesvonhep

BUT WHY DO PEOPLE DIE AND
ARE THEY JUST SLEEPING?

Unfortunately, this section became particularly pertinent as I was writing it, both personally because I began this book shortly after my darling Granny died at the age of 100, but also because Covid-19 has meant we are seeing death rates rise in numbers we wouldn't otherwise have seen in our lifetime.

Though Granny dying was utterly heartbreaking, I felt really lucky to have had the opportunity to speak to Anna Lyons and Louise Winter and draw on their insight during a difficult time. Anna is an end-of-life doula. She supports people who are living with life-limiting illness, their family and friends. Her aim is to help people to live as good a life as possible right up until the very end. Louise Winter is a funeral director who believes that a good funeral can be transformational in helping us acknowledge and accept that someone has died. Together they're the team behind lifedeathwhatever.com.

Anna wrote a wonderful piece for Mother of All Lists on the subject of death and bereavement that I come back to time and time again.[48] It is too long to reproduce here in full (though I do urge you to look it up) but here are some of the most salient points:

- One of the most important lessons is that we need to talk about death.

- We need to plan for it.

- We need to talk openly and honestly to our kids about it.

- We need to embrace the end of life in the same way as we embrace its beginning.

- Death is one true inevitability. There's nothing more certain in this world than mortality.

- Discussing death and dying isn't morbid, or creepy. Done right, it's life-affirming and uplifting.

- Acknowledging mortality does not make you a goth.

- Kids aren't scared of death and dying if they're helped to understand it.

- Thinking the dead dog went to live on a farm doesn't help them. Don't project your own fears onto them. Let kids ask questions and answer them honestly.

- Don't use euphemisms: no, Granddad is not sitting up in the clouds playing tennis with Abraham Lincoln and Great Aunty Marjorie. Euphemisms prevent true understanding. Be straight. Be honest. Be gentle.

- Death and dying need to be a part of our education. As early as children can possibly understand the words.

- We cannot cure death. We can make sure people live as happy a life as possible – right up to the end.

- We need to help those we leave behind. We need to make death into something we can all live well with.

- Grief does not have five stages. Grief is a messy, chaotic splatter of pain and suffering, and each is unique.

- Never ever judge how someone else manages their own grief. Don't assume they're not grieving because they're not doing or saying the things you'd expect.

- Do not judge anyone for 'moving on' quicker than you'd expect. It's not a reflection of the depth of their love for the person who has died.

- The legacy of someone you love lasts a lifetime.
  Be prepared to carry them in head and heart forever.

- Never tell someone they 'should' be 'over it' by now.
  Never.

- When someone you know is grieving, don't be afraid to
  say you have no idea what to say or do. No one expects
  you to.

- 'Disenfranchised grief' describes the grief that society
  doesn't acknowledge. It doesn't make it any less painful or
  tricky. A home, a pet, a celebrity. It's not irrelevant because
  it's not a family member.

- 'Anticipatory grief' is the grief we feel when we know
  someone is going to die. It can also be the fear we are going
  to lose something or someone – even if those feelings aren't
  based in reality. We don't just grieve the life. We grieve lost
  love, lost friendships, the loss of our youth. Grief touches
  much more of our lives than we sometimes realise.

- You never 'get over' someone you love dying. You may
  learn to live with it and without their physical presence,
  but you'll never get over them.

- Say their name.

- Tears are not weakness. It's okay to cry, and there's no
  limit to the tears you're allowed to shed.

- It's okay to make someone cry by talking. You didn't do
  anything wrong.

- Don't tell someone you understand what they're going
  through. Even if you've been through what you think is
  a similar situation. You don't. Every grief is different.
  Don't compare.

- Show up after the funeral flowers have wilted. Set
  reminders to remember birthdays, anniversaries and

important dates. Your life will quickly go back to normal; the bereaved has a new life to forge. Be there for the long haul.

• Make food. Delicious and healthy food that can be put in the freezer.

• Tell them stories of what their loved one meant to you. It's lovely to know the person you loved had an impact on other people too.

• When someone dies, the bond we shared with them doesn't. A mother whose child has died doesn't stop being a mother.

• Remembering and honouring the person who has died doesn't prevent moving on. It can be healing.

• 'Growing around grief' is a lovely model of grief that not enough people know about. Dr Lois Tonkin believes that the grief we feel for someone we really love never gets any smaller and it never diminishes, but the life we carry on living grows around the grief and bolsters and comforts us from it.

• No matter how hard something is to manage, the sun will come up in the morning. Life does go on.

• Grief really does come in waves. Calm seas, followed by huge waves that feel like they'll drown you. If you experience this, try to remember the desperation you are feeling right this second will fade. It will no doubt return, but that'll fade, too.

• You cannot rush grief. Give yourself the time you need, don't ever try to hold yourself to an arbitrary timeline. Think carefully before making life-changing decisions too soon after someone significant to you dies.

• Treats help. Nice things help. Nice people help.

- Never be afraid to ask for help. Never be afraid to ask for company.

- Note to friends: intrude, gently and considerately – keep intruding, frequently and with love. Being there for someone who is grieving isn't an intrusion at all. They might not be 'good company' but include them in your life. When they turn down your nine hundred and ninety-ninth invitation, offer your thousandth. Hold their hand. Walk their path. Help them find their new way.

She concludes with the lovely words: 'In the end, all that really matters is loving and being loved. What do we want at the end? We want to hold; we want to be held. I've never been asked to go get someone's expensive car so they can see it one last time, or to fetch them their Rolex watch. I've never had anyone request "one last e-mail to the CEO to make sure so-and-so has sold those shares".

'I have, however, been asked to help someone see one last sunset, to swim one last time in the ocean, to fall asleep in the arms of their lover, to have their dog come and sit on their bed.

'It's all about love. Real-life human love and the connections we make with them. The mark we leave is imprinted on the hearts and souls of the people we loved unconditionally. In the end, all that really matters is love.'

For me this list was a game-changer and really set a brilliant foundation for how we should be thinking and talking about death.

So to go back to the question for a moment: 'But why do people die and are they just sleeping?'

Short answer: everybody dies, it's part of life. They aren't asleep, they are dead.

Long answer: everybody dies, it's part of life. They aren't asleep, they are dead and here's how to talk about it.

Of course, death, dying and grief are scary subjects because they are linked to losing someone you love and that sucks. That being said, there is so much to be gained from being frank in our conversations around the subject.

Many groups throughout history, from the Buddhists to the Stoics, actively contemplated death to remind them of the impermanence of life.

The phrase 'memento mori' is the Latin for 'remember you are mortal'. That's not to be depressing, it's to give you context.

So how do we go about 'talking death'?

First step. No euphemisms. Every single expert I consulted had this at the top of their list.

While 'kicking the bucket', 'gone to a better place', or 'passed on' might seem like easier options in the short term, they only serve to confuse. If you tell them Granny has passed away or you have 'lost' her, then young children might believe Granny has gone away and be distressed that no one is looking for her, say Anna and Louise.

One euphemism that is often used when talking to kids is equating death to sleep. But kids need to understand that someone has died and that means they'll never come back in their physical form. If you tell them the person is just sleeping, they could a) expect them to wake up and come back, and b) imagine that when they go to sleep they'll die too.

Kids won't be sheltered from these realities when they are older, so the more honest you are about the situation, the more they will be able to cope in the long run.

Makes perfect sense. Question is then, what *do* we tell them and when?

For this I really leaned on the knowledge of Dr Martha Deiros Collado, a clinical psychologist specialising in paediatrics, and children's author and bereavement ambassador, Mark Lemon.

When Mark was twelve years old, his father was murdered, and he has dedicated his adult life to helping children, young people and adults struggling with their grief and mental health.

Lastly, almost everyone I spoke to on this subject recommended the charity Winston's Wish (winstonswish.org) for advice on kids and grief. Imagine how pleased I was when the charity offered to contribute to this book.

It goes without saying that death is a vast and hugely personal subject, but I did spot some themes that came up repeatedly.

Speak, speak, speak some more. If we don't talk, then kids are prone to fill in the gaps themselves, often inaccurately. '[They] are very observant and can have very creative minds; they may overhear conversations or see comments on social media and jump to conclusions about what it means,' says Winston's Wish. 'It is better that they hear the facts of the death, in manageable pieces.'

Mark Lemon agrees: 'I believe it's important that a child is spoken to honestly about what has happened to their loved one. If not communicated to properly, a child can feel a sense of alienation and create their own assumptions about what has happened. When someone special dies, those around the child can feel that the best way not to hurt them is to simply say nothing at all. From my experience, a child wants to feel supported, loved and reassured. Simply asking them if they want to talk, or putting an arm around them during a difficult time, can mean the world to a child or young person struggling with their grief.'

Let them know it's okay to speak about the person who is dead. Encourage conversation by asking the child if there is anything they want to know or if they are unsure about anything. Use age-appropriate language and make it concrete, says Dr Deiros Collado, because children's understanding of the inevitability and permanence of death does not happen until they are seven to nine years old.

This simplified guide that Dr Deiros Collado helped me pull together is a starting point on how to pitch things:

Under the age of three, children will experience death as a separation. Their language skills are not developed enough to understand the word or the meaning behind it.

Between three and six, children do not understand the inevitability and permanence of death but they may see it as something 'special' that can happen. Due to their brain development, they experience 'magical thinking', the idea that things happen by magic or as a punishment. Some might blame themselves or fear they have done 'something bad' to cause it. They do not understand that death is irreversible and may wish to visit Heaven or ask when the person who died will be coming back.

From ages seven to nine, children start to understand that death is final and inevitable but they still won't comprehend that death happens to everyone, including themselves (that happens around puberty). As a result of this new understanding, they may ask lots of questions about death and dying and begin to feel scared about being separated from their parents or carers who are responsible for them.

From ten onwards, children's understanding of death becomes much more real, and as a result they may start to focus more on the biological facts of death and dying. Winston's Wish have also observed that older kids 'might have more queries around the impact of the death on their future'.

The fact is, death and grief are hard to unpick even as adults. Grieving is complex and rarely linear. But there are a few things that might help.

One, flagged by Winston's Wish, is to raise awareness of feelings. 'Often the feelings surrounding grief can be overwhelming for a child and how they respond to these will depend on many factors. To help them along the way it can be useful to name their feelings, let them know it is okay to feel whatever they feel, and help them find a way to manage their difficult feelings. Children often learn from the adults around them and so may look to their behaviour to know how to act themselves.' It might be useful to refer to the 'complex feelings' section (see page 133), which looks in more depth at emotions and learning not to be scared of what you're feeling. Some children might find it hard to express any emotion.

Another thing that might be useful is to remember the importance of play as a tool. Dr Deiros Collado explains it can help children have an outlet to express their emotions and make sense of what is happening. On this topic, I have had some really insightful moments while doing arts and crafts with my kids. Seeing them make cards with love hearts to remember how much they loved their 'Singing Granny' broke my heart, but it was a good way of chatting about our feelings and memories.

Try and pre-empt moments that might be hard, beyond the more obvious ones like Christmas and birthdays. In the short term, many will feel reassured by having their daily routines (mealtimes, sleep and play) kept the same and receiving physical care and affection from someone they know very well and to whom they are strongly attached. On a personal level there is so much value to clinging on to normality when it feels like things are collapsing around you. Similarly, death has a way of making you value mundanity like never before.

Then there's the funeral. I was very unsure about whether to bring our kids to my granny's funeral. My initial reaction was that the kids shouldn't come, that somehow it wasn't appropriate, but I'm so glad we did take them in the end. Not only did it feel like a fitting homage but they behaved impeccably. The funeral was uplifting. They heard each of us talk about her. And they saw the coffin at the end. It gave us all a sense of finality. Death is sad, but it is not scary or to be avoided. And it was okay for them to see me cry.

Of course, whether you feel it's right for your child might depend on the circumstances of the death. But it's fine for them to see adults crying and then for everyone to be okay(ish) afterwards at the wake. You can talk about the notion of happy-sad (see page 143). One crucial point is don't say that the wake is a party, or kids might expect the dead person to be there.

If your child has recently been bereaved, think about how you handle their return to school afterwards. Mark Lemon told me that he found returning to school after his dad died hugely difficult. He remembers struggling to know how to communicate with his friends and teachers about how he was feeling. He suggests: 'A great way to communicate with your teacher is to write on Post-it notes the varied feelings and emotions that you feel on a day-to-day basis. If you're feeling sad in the morning, then give your teacher the sadness Post-it note so your teacher can help you throughout that morning. If your mood changes across the morning, then hand a new Post-it to your teacher at lunchtime.'

All of us (kids included) grieve in our own way and in our own time, and that's okay. There is no set way to coping with death and trauma. Instead, the best thing we can do is allow the child to ask all the questions and communicate how they're feeling in their own time.

When to seek further support (thanks to Winston's Wish):

In the initial months, after the death, it is normal to see a change in behaviour. This may include:

- Difficulties managing emotions
- Risk-taking behaviour
- Soiling, bedwetting, nightmares
- Social isolation/withdrawing from others
- Poor attendance/academic grades dropping

It is important to remember that whilst these behaviours are not exclusively linked to grief, if they continue for prolonged periods of time professional support may be helpful.

Key learnings:

- NEVER EVER use euphemisms to couch or soften the blow.
- Death is unavoidable, so don't hide it from children.
- Expect repetition. Louise and Anna told me that you may need to tell young children several times that someone has died before they really understand. I can definitely relate to that first hand, as in the days and weeks surrounding my granny's death, my kids would say frequently, 'Singing Granny is dead. She's not coming back, is she? Is she dead forever?' Although at first this was hard, sometimes it was

so full-on it made me giggle. But also they were simply saying out loud the same disbelief I was feeling inside. The gut-wrenching impossibility that someone has gone forever.

- Be concrete and consistent with your reply. Even if you've said it many times before, they are trying to wrap their heads around it.

- Be consistent with conversations about pets, as these are often children's first experiences of death.

- Involve them but don't force them to be involved.

- Be truthful and clear but not graphic.

Dealing with grief:

All of this is very well. But death is sad. It's the worst. It is final. And that finality is incomprehensible. And though I am trying to present you with convenient answers, I don't wish to take away from the tragedy of the death of a loved one.

I wanted to offer a bit of insight on grief. Speaking to Cariad Lloyd for *Honestly* was the perfect place to learn about this. Comedian Cariad's dad died of pancreatic cancer when she was fifteen. Her mission is to break the taboo around grief, which led to her award-winning podcast *Griefcast*. After all, she says, 'This is something you're going to have to deal with. This isn't optional.'

As she points out, 'We don't like sadness, it's something we try to avoid at all costs. Our whole world is conditioned to be happy, be positive, to look on the bright side.' This is problematic for many reasons – as we touched on in the section on complex feelings – not least in this instance. Defaulting to joy and optimism doesn't hold up when we are faced with grief. 'Someone's dead,' says Cariad. 'That needs to be shit.'

While we can't magic it better for anyone going through it, whether that be children or adults, we can make sure nobody feels alone with it. Through research for her own book, Cariad discovered that grief lights up the same parts of your brain as depression. And while of course it isn't the same as having a mental-health issue, there are commonalities in how it feels. 'It literally makes you feel like there's no point, no one understands me, I'm isolated, no one cares,' Cariad explains.

We can try to combat that by sharing and connecting, so with that in mind I reached out on Instagram. Of the hundreds of pieces of advice that flooded in, these are the ones that came up time and again:

- Grief can change you as a person.
- It is physically exhausting.
- The sadness affects everything you do.
- Grief affects your brain like 'baby brain'.
- It makes you do strange, out-of-character things, so you should not make major decisions when grieving.
- Grief can make you laugh as well as cry.
- Grieving takes years.
- The process of grief isn't linear; it's long as well as up and down.
- It can feel like you are learning to live again.
- Grief doesn't end.
- No two losses are the same.
- There is never enough time.
- Anticipatory grief is a thing.
- When someone dies, it doesn't erase them from your lives.

- One day your life will feel brighter again.

- There will be good days and bad days. And you shouldn't feel guilty about enjoying life when you can.

How, then, can we help someone who is grieving?

- Say the dead person's name.

- Don't dismiss their feelings. Acknowledge how shit it is.

- Don't ask what you can do to help. They won't have the capacity to think about it. Just do it.

- Send the text, write the letter, make the call. Even 'thinking of you' means the world and there's no such thing as too much kindness.

- Never say 'Everything happens for a reason'.

- It is rarely better for the person left behind that someone is gone.

- Living to a good age doesn't stop the loss being painful.

- Just be normal. Too many people avoid those who are grieving.

- Don't worry about getting it right. Just be there.

- Let them tell the story. Share yours too.

- Don't try to fix the problem.

- Don't compare your grief.

- Just because a year has gone by (or more) doesn't mean they are okay.

And one final thing that I often come back to is the 'ball in the box' theory, famously posted on Twitter by Lauren Herschel after her doctor shared it with her.

The idea is that grief is like a ball in a box. On the inside of the box is a pain button. To begin with, the grief-ball is so huge it takes up most of the box, so it hits the pain button constantly.

For most people the grief-ball never disappears, but it does shrink. Which means that day to day it doesn't activate the pain button, but when it does it is just as hard as ever, plus it can be unexpected, which is tough.

Not only is this idea a brilliant articulation of something that can feel so complex, it's one that kids can understand too. You can't make it go away, so you need to talk about it. Even if you don't know what to say, just acknowledge that it is hard to talk about, and that's a good place to start.

Remember we aren't supposed to be experts in grief. Even those who have offered insight to this section are just trying hard to figure out the unknowable.

This might be a bizarre thing to say, but none of us knows what the dying part of death is like and this 'unknowing-ness' adds an extra dimension when attempting to answer questions; because death is in fact the ultimate 'unanswered question' at the end of every life.

Though we may not know what death is like, we can work to stop making it 'off limits'. Talk about death, share our experiences, say the words we want to say to those we love. And also take peace from something I heard Alain de Botton say on Elizabeth Day's *How to Fail* podcast. He said people worry about the dead, but we have to remember the dead are okay. Because they are already dead. I find this weirdly reassuring. Dead people aren't sleeping. But they are okay.

BUT WHY DO YOU BELIEVE IN GOD?

Hmmmmm. Do I believe in God? I genuinely don't know. I was raised in a Christian home. Our local village church was a significant part of my childhood and also where Ben and I got married.

Truthfully I can't decide if we did it because of God or because of the deep connection I felt to that building: Christmas mornings spent at the 8.30 a.m. service, willing the time to go by so I could get home to open my presents. Being bridesmaid at my aunty's wedding. Sitting in the front pew during my granny and then grandpa's funerals. School trips to look at the gravestones, and local conspiracy theories that if you lifted a particular stone from the top of a particular monument you would unleash a bad spirit on the whole village. (Can you imagine how horrifying/appealing that is to a bunch of eight-year-olds on a school trip?)

Yes, I feel deeply connected to Holy Trinity Church in Drayton Parslow. And maybe that feeling of being connected – both to previous generations, my own heritage and also to my local community – is what it's all about?

As I have got older, the idea of God has been less resonant. Though I would love to have a clear-cut faith as my grandparents did, I find it increasingly difficult to reconcile the concept of belief in the divine with friends dying of cancer in their thirties, or infertility after baby loss.

Instead, I find comfort in the abstract sense of 'The Universe'. In thinking that I am a tiny part of a much bigger picture. That it is vital to try to be a good, kind, thoughtful member of both the community and society.

How would you describe God?

During my research, 53 per cent of the 5,000 people I asked told me they believed in God. Yet only 45 per cent of respondents were linked to a religion.

A few people said God was 'unexplainable'. However, those who did have the words saw God in the following way: '*A creator, saviour and guide . . . All-knowing. All-seeing . . . Comforting, caring, guiding . . . My source of peace . . . A higher power . . . A greater energy.*'

Other answers included: '*Constant consciousness . . . A faith/ belief in something . . . An eternal spirit outside of our energy . . . Omnipresent . . . Something bigger than us/me . . . Caretaker . . . Karma.*' (I sometimes like to think this, but good things do happen to bad people and vice versa.)

Lots of people cited nature/the idea of Mother Nature, which appeals to me because when I'm looking at the sea or the mountains, that is the time when I feel most grounded to my place in the world. Or the changing seasons.

Extreme answers included: *God is my reason for everything, the single most important thing in my life.* Terrifying answer: *God is watching what we humans do when left to our own devices.*

'Love' was another overwhelmingly popular answer. One person messaged about having a sense of longing when they thought of God. Not feeling drawn to a religion, but wanting the access to community that it brings.

'I believe in science,' said one respondent. 'But I don't believe it is over when we die.'

What does your belief give you?

The answers to this were varied. '*Appreciation, focus, accept-ance . . . A moral compass and guidance . . . Perspective . . . Reassurance . . . Hope . . . Confidence and trust . . . Faith in myself . . . Connectedness to all beings and the planet . . . A framework to process the big stuff . . . Salvation . . . It grounds and humbles me . . . Trust in allowing life to unfold rather than gripping it with white knuckles . . . An ability to hand over and see myself humbly . . . Hope in a world that can sometimes feel hopeless . . . Peaceful answers to scary thoughts . . . Unconditional community . . . Strength in hard times . . . Community and the opportunity to celebrate life's milestones . . . A reminder that everything has a purpose.*'

There were negative answers too. '*It doesn't give me much . . . A belief in causality as opposed to a faith in supremacy . . . It lands me with guilt and a set of morals I'm not always sure about.*'

God in relation to death seemed popular. Hope that the end is not the end. That you can still feel the presence of an absent loved one.

How to answer the question, 'But why do you believe in God?'

Here's a selection of possible answers to children that my respondents came up with:

- I would explain that I don't, but it is important that we learn about and respect all beliefs.

- I don't. But there are lots of different gods and you can choose one when you grow up.

- Yes, but not always, and it's okay to have changing views.

- No, but would you like to learn together? Open the discussion.

- No. I am humanist. We have one life and we should live it as best we can.

- I don't know. It's something I am still thinking about. Do you?

- I would talk about beliefs and what they mean.

The main thing that came up more than once is that religion is deeply personal and nobody should push beliefs or have them pushed on them. Several respondents resented having religion forced upon them as a child.

Researching this briefly took me down a path of trying to explain heaven, specifically the chances of proving its existence. Errrrr, word of advice: this is melon-twisting stuff. But it did point me towards the late astronomer Carl Sagan and his wife Ann Druyan and the work they have done on the tension between religion and science.

Sagan wanted us to see ourselves as *starstuff*, made of atoms forged in the fiery hearts of distant stars and 'organised assemblages of 10 billion billion billion atoms considering the evolution of atoms; tracing the long journey by which, here at least, consciousness arose'. For him, science was, in part, a kind of 'informed worship'.[49]

Ann Druyan talks about a level of spirituality that can be found in the fact that we are the product of 13 billion years of cosmic evolution. And that for her, the community and connectivity required for us to evolve is almost a religious notion.

Still confused? Me too. But I like the idea of the magic within science.

In conclusion? It's very complicated. All of the above answers are amazing, but they are also hugely abstract. The more I have delved into it, the more I have come to think that our belief systems are something we have to find for ourselves.

In these moments it's handy to default to some facts: a religion is a set of beliefs that is held by a bunch of people.

These beliefs are then linked to a supernatural being or God. The biggest religions are Christianity, Islam, Hinduism, Buddhism, Taoism, Sikhism and Judaism. There are many other religions.

You could then extend it to explain that people who do not believe in any gods are called atheists and people who are not sure whether they believe or not are called agnostics.

Then if you want to dig deeper, ideally without confusing things, you might chat about humanists who reject the idea of a supernatural god altogether; for them it's about having a 'non-religious belief system' which is focused around human welfare and the idea that there is just the one life and world.

And then there's the broader scope of 'spirituality', which might not have set gods or rules and may for some not feel like it belongs here. The difference between that and religion is that religions are based on a set of organised beliefs and practices, whereas spirituality is more of a personal belief system.

This is a vast and fascinating topic with lots to consider, but here are some key learnings I picked up along the way:

- Explore many religions. There are great things we can learn from one another's beliefs.

- Talk about the place for science. Turns out it can be magic too.

- You can be passionate about your beliefs but that shouldn't mean persuasive.

- To have faith is not set in stone. It's changeable, just as we change.

- Faith is neither inherently bad or good. It's how it feels for the person that matters.

- Be honest about your own beliefs (or that you aren't sure).

- Ask your kid what they think. Mine already have great knowledge about other religions and love chatting about who or what God is! (Kids' brains are so cool, aren't they?!)

If all else fails, remember this Yoko Ono quote: 'My religion is to trust myself.' And also the wise words of a nine-year-old I spoke to who said: 'Religion is people trying to find answers to questions they can't answer.' Sounds about right, and also very apt, as we wind towards the end.

BUT WHY DO WE HAVE 'LOVE'?

I am taking this one to mean 'what is love?' Unfortunately, I made the mistake of googling this and was reminded of the Haddaway track ('Baby, don't hurt me . . .'), released in 1993 when I was eleven and yet to really have a clue about the complexity of love. I hadn't even fallen head over heels for Robbie Williams by that point . . .

Looking to music seems as good a place as any to begin: love is all around us. Love is all you need. All of me loves all of you. Love lifts us up where we belong.

Okay, this didn't get me any closer to the answer.

Reading around the subject, there seems to be some central ideas to land for kids. The first is that love is infinite, so there is enough for everyone.

Next, give them solid examples of people and things they love. Here it might also be useful to draw on Zick Rubin's 'Scales of Liking and Loving', which was seen as a breakthrough bit of research back in 1970 (but once you read it sounds really obvious). Rubin believed you can be 'in like' with someone (that sounds odd, doesn't it?), which might mean appreciation or admiration, but the difference is that when you are 'in love' you find yourself caring as much about the other person's needs as your own. That makes a lot of sense to me. And it's a good barometer of the special people in my life whom I am definitely more than 'in like' with.

From here on in, things get more abstract; so much so that I sought answers far and wide from those who seemed well versed in the subject.

The musician Nick Cave frames love as 'seeing someone'. Observing all that they are. Which goes back to the idea of wholeness. Love means we accept someone as they are, including the bits that they might otherwise fear make them unloveable.

Psychotherapist Esther Perel (my go-to gospel on anything marriage-related) talks about how we have been sold the glamourised version of love as exciting, whereas at its best, love is safe and occasionally boring. She describes how there is a tension between our need for security versus our desire for freedom, and how we must look to find the middle ground: giving ourselves wholeheartedly, but with a sense of separateness.

The School of Life asks us to consider that the first type of love we encounter is one we experience in childhood, usually from our parents. Which hopefully (but sadly not always) feels unconditional, simple and one-sided, with all our needs met. The notion of love in that context is it's the thing that makes us feel whole. Love is a feeling of completeness.

While the internet's favourite grandparents, Pauline and Geoffrey Walker (@geoffreywalk), who have been married for seventy years, tell us that love is the feeling that you can't wait to meet that person again.

That's just the tip of the iceberg. This is a selection of definitions of love that people shared via Instagram. They completed the sentence 'Love is . . .'

- Complicated.
- Not what you expect it to be.
- Powerful.
- An invisible line connecting two people.
- Compromise.

- Calm.

- Like coming home.

- Caring about someone's happiness more than your own.

- Unexplainable.

- Often unexpected.

- Striving to be better for another person.

- Something that gives you a sense of acceptance.

- It is hard work but worth it.

- Something that takes commitment.

- It's a pain in the arse.

- It's trust.

- It's absolute peace and chaos.

- A beautiful struggle.

- It's about respect, gratitude, partnership, listening, learning.

- Giving someone your last mouthful of food.

- Accepting someone as they are, being seen.

- A whole load of contradictions, all-consuming (and that isn't always a good thing).

- Not always easy but shouldn't be so hard it hurts. It's sometimes not enough.

There is bags of wisdom there but there was one answer that came back repeatedly: *Love is not a fairytale.* Yes. Yes. Yes.

When we hear 'what is love?' it's easy to think of the image that Hollywood paints – a sparkly, firework-filled experience; masses of red roses, glorious sunsets, popping champagne. The world stops turning the moment you clap eyes on each other.

The reality (for most) is very different. Sure, there is fizz and excitement. Short term it can have a chemical effect, even with a platonic friendship. That vibe when you find a new friend, or have a bit of banter with a work colleague. It can feel electric and thrilling.

Now I am not wanting to piss on any parades. Love is wonderful. Who wouldn't want to wish for their children the kind of love that you want to shout from the rooftops? Yet while it should feel amazing, it should also be mellow and easy and uncomplicated. Exciting but not unsafe. Joyous but not out of control. Love shouldn't feel like a need.

So what else do we want to arm our kids with? This is some more of the wisdom I accrued from the people I surveyed. **Things I want to teach my kids about love:**

- To embrace it, but don't lose who you are.

- That it is as important to love another as it is to be loved.

- Love whoever you want, as long as they respect you. If it doesn't feel right, it's not love.

- It takes work.

- Welcome its arrival and nurture its endurance.

- It's not the same as sex.

- That their parents love them unconditionally no matter what.

- That it has highs and lows.

- That 'almost love' isn't good enough.

- Love exists in all sorts of relationships.

- Love and being in love are different.

- You can't make anyone love you.

- Non-romantic love is as valuable as romantic love.

- Never feel you have to love someone.

- It's also important to be happy on your own.

Love isn't always plain sailing, though, is it? When asked if they thought there were any downsides to love, 91 per cent of those who responded said there were (which begs the question, who are the other 9 per cent?!). Here are some of my respondents' thoughts on these downsides:

- We will all experience heartbreak at some point.

- When you love someone, you take on their worries, hopes and concerns.

- It can cloud your judgement, and cause the exhausting fear of losing someone. Grief is the price we pay for love.

- Parental love is having your heart outside of your body.

So, heartbreak is utterly grim – but is it a worthy exchange for love? Sometimes. Each love that I have had, even after it ended, has shaped me. I have grown because of it.

The importance of self-love:

We have touched on bursting the myth of 'Disneyfied' love. Part of that means there ain't no prince or princess coming to save you. Instead, the thing that can ride in on a white horse is self-love (nope, you're right, that analogy doesn't work at all, but hey ho).

There wasn't such a thing as self-love or self-care when I was growing up. Now this concept is often thrown about a little too liberally. When I say self-care I am not talking about bubble baths and facemasks, though they are undoubtedly lovely; what I mean is looking out for and being responsible for your own needs.

During her TED Talk, author Chidera Eggerue calls for us to move on from the idea that a) romance and marriage are the ultimate achievement, and b) (at the other end of the pendulum) solitude is something to be feared.[50]

She is spot on! What's more admirable is learning to revel in your own company. Rather than searching out companionship or for someone else to 'love' you and provide happiness, focus on doing that for yourself. Whoever told us that the world doesn't revolve around us was actually incorrect. I am not advocating selfishness, but the truth is you are your one true constant; it is your responsibility to take excellent care of yourself.

The best thing is, it's cyclical too. Self-love benefits others – the more you understand and embrace what makes you you, the better positioned you are to do the same for others.

Okay, so if self-love is meeting or exceeding your own needs, what do we want to teach our kids about how we show love? These are some of the answers I got when I asked this question:

- Forgiveness and acceptance.

- Being honest.

- Being kind without expecting anything in return.

- Listening.

- Selflessness. (This made me recoil. Not sure I agree! Do you?)

- Holding hands and hugging.

- Small gestures like making tea in the morning.

- Honesty (yes!).

- Being there and showing up – over and over again.

One thing to note here is, perhaps surprisingly, nobody talked about showing love in terms of buying flowers or fancy trips. Those things are the 'icing on the cake'.

Showing love runs much deeper than that; it is the intent behind the action. When you pick a gift for someone it doesn't matter if it costs £5 or £50, it's the thought process of finding something that you hope they will like that counts.

I would also add something to that list: love is helping someone be the best, most fulfilled and content version of themselves. Love is about caring enough about someone that you want the best outcome for them, and sometimes that means choosing options that are tough. That can mean a bunch of less pretty and cute but nonetheless valuable things: holding each other accountable, having difficult conversations, respecting one another's need to be on their own, making and saying sorry for mistakes. They aren't the bits you'll see in the movies but I believe they make for the most fulfilling relationships. Love for me is directly linked to honesty.

Lastly but definitely not 'leastly', the best way to show someone you love 'em is to tell them.

I hope my children have love in many forms. Finding a soulmate is wonderful. But I don't believe it should be the be-all and end-all. What about the love for friends? For pets? For neighbours? For your home? Your siblings? Every type of love is wonderful and valuable. Never take someone's love for granted. Having someone love you in any form is a gift. As such, I have made a real habit of telling people I love them. It started with my husband and then my kids. Then I extended it to friends and siblings. If you know you love someone, tell them! Better to have been a person who loved too much, than not enough.

I tell them: 'I am here.' Love challenges the inner fear of loneliness. I see this brought to life really powerfully with my kids via one simple trick. Whenever they are upset, and especially if it's fuelled by shame or embarrassment or guilt, I squeeze them extra tight and say, 'I am here and I love you.' Something about saying 'I am here' makes them instantly relax.

Similarly, I love it when someone texts to say: 'Here if you need me.' So simple but so grounding. I guess it's a verbal reminder that you are worthy of love even at the moments when you feel unloveable. In fact, especially in these moments. Whatever the problem is, we are not alone.

What a question to end on. Most people think of love as romantic love. But as I've been writing I am consumed by parental love. This is a love like no other. The one that turned me and my world upside down and inside out. That showed me quite literally that the hardest job in the world can also be the best.

That's the beauty of it. Love provides answers to questions you didn't know you needed answering. It is uncertain and undefinable.

I could dedicate a whole book to the subject of love but a) I am very aware that the best writers in history have already tried and not successfully or succinctly articulated it, and b) I would still be no closer to an answer, which brings me seamlessly on to my last musing . . . the power of not knowing.

JOINING BIT SEVEN:

THE IMPORTANCE OF NOT KNOWING

Vulnerability is not knowing victory or defeat;
it's understanding the necessity of both, it's
engaging. It's being all in.[51]

Brené Brown

I am a huge fan of Brené Brown – okay, that is an understatement. Hearing her speak about the notion of vulnerability being a superpower, and that embracing your weakness is courageous, was game-changing for me.

Brené's research on vulnerability affirmed for me that when things make me feel wobbly that is okay; in fact, it's probably a good sign – it's where the growth and the big stuff happens.

Her theories can also be applied to the context of answering challenging questions from your children. Sometimes this means admitting you don't know. Perhaps that might feel shameful, or embarrassing. But not so! It's showing that you are human.

It's something that Alain de Botton touched on when I spoke to him about 'emotional wellness'. One thing that really stayed with me was when he said that most parents house a deep-seated fear that we are going to screw up our kids. Yet our actual role is not to be perfect or impenetrable, it's to introduce them lovingly and safely to the reality of adult life. The sooner we can plant the seed we aren't perfect, it teaches them they're not perfect either and that's all the better. Being human means being fundamentally flawed and that's what's so great about it. It means there is always something to learn.

I have a tendency to try to control. I like a plan; I like to research; I'm not averse to a schedule, a system or a process. That way you know where you are at, right? In many ways, yes. But we also need to allow for flexibility. In meditative practice, they talk about holding a bird in the hand – you need to find a way to keep it secure without squashing it. It's about having systems, but not defaults you can't deviate from. If you aren't prepared to be flexible then how are you going to grow?

Being certain doesn't allow for nuance. Not knowing isn't about ignorance. It's about being smart enough to know when we don't know. Confident enough to be unsure.

Better to have no opinion and be willing to explore it than to be completely rigid in an answer you've not taken the time to consider. As Marcus Aurelius said: 'You always own the option of having no opinion.'

Similarly, when I spoke to Ovie Soko, professional basketball player turned author of *You Are Dope*,[52] he said something that really stayed with me. When you look at a situation (in this case answering questions), be conscious of the fact that there are no right answers on your path, because you are the only one to have trodden it. You can seek wisdom from other people's paths, but yours is yours.

What I now realise is that this parenting lark is about trying to prepare my children for unknowable experiences outside of my own.

It's also worth noting that not only is there no such thing as 'knowing it all', but if there was, would you actually want it? Remember at school when you didn't really like the 'know-it-all' kid? Which is a bit mean, because they were probably okay really. Maybe. But a know-it-all needs a reality check. Self-righteousness blocks conversation. Believing you are right is the opposite of the reality; nobody is always right. Because more often than not, 'right' doesn't exist; there are several versions of right and several versions of wrong. And even, confusingly, several versions of 'on the fence'. All of which are valuable.

There is great humility in saying 'I don't know'. Be brave enough to sit with not having a clue. Be gracious enough to admit, 'I didn't know that, thanks for telling me.' Be humble enough to say, 'I don't know yet, but I am figuring it out.'

In Zen Buddhism they talk about *shoshin*, a word meaning 'beginner's mind'. It refers to having an attitude of openness, eagerness, and lack of preconceptions when studying a subject, even when studying at an advanced level, just as a beginner would.

When I was a kid, I had this idea that as soon as I got to a certain age I would have figured it all out: when I'm a teenager I'll 'get it', when I get to uni I will figure it out, or when I become a mum I'll have things nailed.

Now I understand that I'll still be saying that when I am a granny. There's always stuff to learn. There are always unanswered questions. The world is changing. You are changing. Every time you think you've worked it all out, it'll change again (very much like parenting).

Next time one of my three kids lands me a really tricky, sticky question, I am going to take pleasure and pride in saying, 'I don't know. Do you? Shall we try to figure it out together?'

It feels like holding each other's hands and going on an adventure. And of course there's always the possibility that they have the answer, not us!

When I was a kid, I wish I had known that . . .
love, marriage and then babies didn't necessarily
go in that order.

Natalie Duvall @dopeblackmums

'WHAT DO I WISH I HAD KNOWN
AS A KID?'

The nuggets from this line of enquiry were so brilliant that I began to ask everyone and anyone (which sounds really extreme until we remember that I was writing this during a pandemic, and so for several months the only people I saw were my family and the people I bumped into around Peckham).

However, here are some of the best answers:

I wish I had known that I could be whoever I wanted and do and live wherever I want and that is not difficult. That school hierarchy doesn't translate into the real world; eating crusts doesn't make your hair curly; naps are cool; love isn't a fairytale; and I should keep my handpainted Doctor Marten boots as they will come back in fashion. That my parents stopping me doing what I wanted was because they loved me; that happiness is an inside job; that being weird is excellent. I wish I had known less; that failing at something is not the end, it can be the beginning; that you should say yes more than no. That you don't have to eat all your food if you are full; life is hard but that is part of it; you won't feel like an adult when you become one; childhood is short; brushing your teeth is important; being sensitive is okay; not getting married is an option; and confident people don't necessarily know more. I wish I had known that you can rely on yourself; a job and a career are not the same thing; life is about love; parents don't know everything; and cutting your own fringe is never ever a good idea.

BUT WHY?

What would mine be? Can I just steal all of the above? For me it would have been to stop trying to have all the answers (and stop trying to be too grown-up) and to be comfortable with figuring it out. That's probably my answer to my adult self too.

CONCLUSION

What did I hope to achieve with this book?

Short answer: find answers to tricky questions.

Longer answer or 'desired outcome' (if you wanna get a little more fancy): to engage with my kids in a way that would feed curiosity, nurture an open mind and provide knowledge, but maintain innocence without allowing them to be naïve. Which in turn taught me that I needed to be curious and to learn too.

Truthful answer/reality: am I allowed to swear?! Ha! Fuckkkkkkkkkkkkkkkkk.

Many times I felt I'd bitten off more than I could chew; both in terms of trying to raise three children well, but also trying to write this book.

Not only that, but how could I possibly do justice to all the hundreds of stories I've had access to via Mother of All Lists, the hours of conversation with experts on my *Honestly* and *But Why?* podcasts and years of chatting to people from all walks of life, thanks to social media? And how could I process them in a way that did justice to the honour of having this wealth of human experience and insight to share?

Good news is (on the parenting part), it isn't just me: as I mentioned in the intro, 87 per cent of 2,000 people I surveyed worried about answering these questions 'wrong'. Not having the words, not knowing how to pitch stuff appropriately, questioning their own knowledge and bias.

Second good news: I found some handy 'ways in' to approaching the 'but why?'s which momentarily controlled my panic. Here are three of them:

✳ 1) Remember yourself as a child ✳

For me as for everyone, 2020 has been a time of huge reflection. One huge trigger was sorting out my granny's house after her death. She had kept so many pictures and letters I had drawn for her as a child. They gave me such a great reminder of who I was as a child. And then I found this note to my younger brother and sister:

> *Dear Susie and Charlie,*
> *Please will you sit next to me at breakfast?*
> *Love Clemmie xxxxxxxxxxxxxxx*

The paper was scrappy and the writing scrawly. And it broke my heart. Partly because Granny had kept it for thirty-odd years, but also because it made me wonder – why wouldn't I want to sit on my own?

I like to think that perhaps there was something I particularly wanted to chat to the others about? Sadly I don't remember the back story, so instead tried to imagine what was going through my head when I wrote this: what did seven-year-old Clemmie need? And I don't mean in relation to that breakfast circa 1989 – I mean what did she 'theoretically' need in the moment when asking her family questions?

- To be heard.

- To be able to ask freely.

- To see parents' actions match up to their words.

- To receive truthful answers – even if that's simply 'I don't know'.

- To be encouraged to keep learning.

Remember when you were a kid and you really wanted to go to a theme park and go on all the rides? And your parents weren't up for it. Or at least mine weren't. I literally could NOT comprehend it. Why wouldn't you want to have all the fun?

Then I became the adult and now I detest theme parks. But when answering these questions, I try to dispel my logical, grown-up, sensible conclusions and provide answers that match the excited desire for the world that little me would have wanted. Tell them how it is, but leave cynicism at the door.

2) Work on your answering techniques

Between questions, in the 'joining bits', I looked into some of the ways to try to improve the art of working out your answers to the big questions. To recap, they were:

- A window of silence as per Erling Kagge – and if that seems laughably ambitious, simply try to factor in some quiet and reflection amongst all the to-do.

- The importance of conversation and indeed listening. Answering questions isn't about playing Google – it's an opportunity to truly engage with your kids, to chew the fat. Sometimes they just want your undivided attention (gulp). It's easy to forget but they are curious about your mind and want you to be curious about theirs.

- Judge yourself, not others. Energy spent worrying what others are up to or indeed gossiping is not time well spent. I'd argue it's actually a waste of time, not least because none of us knows what anyone else is going through. Instead use your energy to work on being a more informed version of yourself.

- Think about thinking. Sometimes it's a process, which can be very uncomfortable, but that doesn't mean it's wrong.

- Be honest (nearly) always. With yourself and with your kids.

- Tune in to the power of intuition and, bigger picture, demonstrate living in line with your own beliefs.

- And lastly, most importantly, there is the huge significance of not knowing! That's not a failing – that's a superpower.

3) Have an honest conversation with yourself

Over and over again I have felt like we all share a desire, but are stuck with the same problem. Namely: everybody wants the answers, but nobody is willing to learn. So the first step towards doing that is to have an honest conversation with yourself.

When answering anything, ask yourself:

- Where have I got this answer from?

- Is this something that I truly think or is it acquired knowledge?

- Is it the best version of the answer I can give?

- Is it loaded with any potential bias?

- Could the answer be wrong?

- What does the opposite opinion look like and is there value in that?

- If I haven't got an answer, is it because I am opting out of a challenge or an uncomfortable chat?

- Am I willing to put the work in to find the answers?

Now that's a lot. And I am (very) realistic. One of my kids asked me a series of big questions while I was trying to blow up an airbed inside a tent. It was thirty-five degrees, I was sweaty and hungry and in the throes of PMT. With the best will in the world, he wasn't going to get a considered answer at that moment.

That checklist isn't meant to be, well, a checklist – ha! More an example of the value of really, truly interrogating your thoughts.

What else? Is it a bit punchy to call for the death of 'middle talk'? Maybe. Gonna do it anyway. What is middle talk, you might ask? It's not small talk – that can be fun and insightful. For example, asking someone what is their favourite smell can lead to some excellent chat (mine is clothes dried in the sun).

And it's not a big, proper chat either (as you can tell, I love those).

Middle talk is the filler stuff: the 'did you have a good week-end?', 'weather is rubbish, isn't it?', 'off anywhere nice?' The throwaway bits of chat that are nothing more than perfunctory and inspire minimum connection between those involved. If we are going to talk then let's go for it! Having a chat with another human is such a great opportunity to learn.

While we are here and I am making outlandish requests, can we agree to try and chill out on the tech too? Answers at our fingertips, voices that shout loudly on social media, screens that clutter mealtimes. Let's put some shackles on it. Demanding, I know! But I feel we are in an era that demands we do something, and as such I want to close with a note on the bigger picture.

Also: 2020. The year of years. The rollercoaster ride that taught us that everything we thought we knew to be certain and true no longer was. When is our next holiday? What does going to work look like? What's the best way to behave now? Where can I look for advice? No definitive answers.

I can't decide if it was a blessing or a curse that the proposal for this book was out for pitch as we locked down. I often wonder what shape this book would have taken had I not been writing it largely in isolation.

The other thing I can't tell is whether my long and drawn-out existential crisis has occurred because of the book or because of the times we are living in. My guess is it's a bit of both. But one thing I do know for sure is that when as a nation, or indeed as humans, we are all moving through something that has never happened before, then the reality is: THERE ARE NO CONVENIENT ANSWERS.

That person on Instagram hasn't got the answers. The person WhatsApping articles to you hasn't got the answers. The woman from the village's second cousin's aunty doesn't have the answer. At times it's been clear that those in power haven't got any answers either! Which is uncomfortable and disconcerting. But it is what it is.

Covid-19 has been a horrendous experience, first because of the loss of lives and devastating effect on the economy, but also because it has plunged us into a global sense of uncertainty.

And not knowing is something we aren't used to any more. In this instance it's useful to a) accept things as they are, or b) look for answers in different places.

Remember, there is rarely one finite solution, nor only one way to find answers. Not least because there are three different kinds of wisdom – acquired, intellectual and experiential. Though you may be abundant in one you may well be lacking in the other. That's okay. The discomfort of not knowing is the catalyst for learning.

Easier said than done. As well as feeling out of control about life (standard 2020 stuff), I was also a ball of anxiety that I was hugely under-qualified to write this book. Yet in rational moments, and backed by learnings from hours of research, I began to truly understand that even the experts are qualified in only one bit of the big picture: the clinical sexologist, for example, is amazing on the subject of erections but at a loss when it comes to environmentalism.

Dr Liz O'Riordan, the consultant breast surgeon mentioned in the chapter about cancer, wrote an amazing piece about how she assumed she knew what breast cancer was like because she had operated on many others who suffered from it. She assumed she knew what it was like to have a mastectomy because she had advised many other women. But all of what she 'thought she knew' went out the window when she received her own breast cancer diagnosis. An expert is still a human at the end of the day.

There is no hierarchy. Nobody has the answers. But we all have the ability to keep asking questions. Without judgement of ourselves.

In fact, it sounds counterintuitive but I'd say this: if life feels like it's throwing up more questions than it's answering, then you are getting it right. If you feel unsure and uncomfortable and, most importantly, if the not-knowing inspires you to keep learning rather than switch off, then you are doing the right thing.

BUT WHY?

As the saying goes: remember our thoughts generate words, words generate actions, actions generate habits, habits generate character, and character breeds destiny. This book was never about the answers; it was an opportunity to ask questions – of ourselves, as parents, of our children and of the world around us. To use them as a route to discovery. It was never 'But why?' It was more a case of 'But why not?'

ACKNOWLEDGEMENTS

How weird to be writing this part! A big thank you to: my book agent Jane, to Lindsey, Kate, Lindsay, Alara, Ellie and the rest of the crew at Headline Home and all the Tape Agency family. I'm very lucky to have you all on my side; you make everything feel easier, even when the world has been imploding around us.

Emma – I'm in awe of your talent and patience as a designer and all-round excellence as a human. Anna Mathur, thank you for writing the foreword; it's been an honour and a lifeline to have been sailing/flailing through things together.

All the following people who always have my back: Jane, Niran, Ali, Charlie, Gemma, Tash, Ria, Hollie D-C, Zoe S, Glorious Bitches, Wolf Sisters, Ski Ergggg – you da best.

Team TYP (especially Gareth, Kelly and Charlie) – did I mention I have written a book? I pictured 'authoring' in a cottage in the countryside, but give me a warehouse in Peckham any day. Thank you for keeping me fit and sane and ensuring there is zero chance of me getting too big for my boots thanks to the near-constant piss-taking.

Zade – **warning, compliment incoming** – this would have been a very different book without you. Not sure you knew what you were getting yourself into, but I am eternally grateful that you did.

The Hags: Laura, Rowan, Polly – who'd have predicted that you could fall more in love with your best friends after twenty years? There's nobody I would rather be growing old with. Given the choice, I would always choose you three.

To my family – prolifically complex, unendingly supportive and the people who taught me to overthink everything (ideally while also devouring good food). Wonder how many of you will actually bother to read it? YES, this is a test.

Ben – wow, you really did pick up the pieces. Thank you for giving me the opportunity to fulfil one of my dreams. I love you and appreciate all that you do for our family. Even if I don't say it often enough.

My darling Granny – I frequently imagine being able to tell you that I am a published author. I hope you would be very proud. You are my sunshine and my guiding light.

Bertie, Woody and Greta – even though you have told me categorically that 'this sounds like a very boring book'. You are forever my greatest achievement. When I am searching for answers, you three provide them for me in spades. I love you so much it hurts.

Anyone who has bought, liked, listened to, commented on or contributed to anything I have put out on the internet – it's a privilege and an honour to have people hear what you have to say, and one that I never take for granted.

2020 – the year of all years. You came. You turned life upside down, but somehow you gave me a book to show for it.

ENDNOTES

1 Huie, Jessica, *Purpose: Find Your Truth and Embrace Your Calling*, Hay House, 2018
2 Perry, Philippa, *The Book You Wish Your Parents Had Read (and Your Children Will be Glad That You Did)*, Penguin Life, 2019
3 Jeffers, Oliver, *Here We Are: Notes for Living on Planet Earth*, HarperCollins, 2017
4 https://metro.co.uk/2020/07/27/dope-black-mums-how-talk-children-about-racism-13042492/
5 Tatum, Beverly Daniel, *Can We Talk About Race? And Other Conversations in an Era of School Resegregation*, Beacon Press, 2008
6 https://www.tolerance.org/print/66643
7 https://motherofalllists.com/2018/05/21/how-finally-learned-to-be-kind-to-myself/
8 https://motherofalllists.com/2018/06/25/dwarfism-and-what-it-means-to-be-different/
9 Hill, Maisie, *Period Power*, Bloomsbury, 2019
10 https://kids.britannica.com
11 https://www.voicesofyouth.org/blog/masculinity-and-femininity
12 https://www.ted.com/talks/susannah_temko_what_it_means_to_be_intersex?
13 https://www.plannedparenthood.org/learn/parents/preschool/how-do-i-talk-with-my-preschooler-about-identity
14 https://www.nationalgeographic.com/magazine/2017/01/how-science-helps-us-understand-gender-identity/
15 Sandstrom, Gillian, and Dunn, Elizabeth, 'Social Interactions and Well-Being: The Surprising Power of Weak Ties', *Personality and Social Psychology Bulletin*, 1 July 2014
16 The School of Life, and Stewart, Lizzy, *Happy, Healthy Minds: A Children's Guide to Emotional Wellbeing*, The School of Life Press, 2020
17 Whitehouse, Anna and Farquharson, Matt, *Where's My Happy Ending? Happily Ever After and How the Heck to Get There*, Bluebird, 2020
18 Ransom, Amy, *The Soul-Soaring Virtues of Separation*, Hay House UK, 2021
19 https://motherofalllists.com/2018/02/12/life-after-divorce/

20 https://motherofalllists.com/2017/10/27/guest-list-surviving-divorce/

21 Mathur, Anna, *Mind Over Mother: Every Mum's Guide to Worry and Anxiety in the First Years*, Piatkus, 2020

22 https://motherofalllists.com/2019/01/18/quit-the-comparison/

23 Stixrud, Dr William, and Johnson, Ned, *The Thriving Child: The Science Behind Reducing Stress and Nurturing Independence*, Penguin Life, 2018

24 Syed, Matthew, 'How to Raise a Happy Child – What Every Parent Needs to Know', *The Times*, 4 September 2020

25 Maddox, Lucy, *Blueprint: How Our Childhood Makes Us Who We Are*, Robinson, 2018

26 https://motherofalllists.com/2020/05/15/how-our-childhood-makes-us-who-we-are/

27 https://www.ted.com/talks/lucinda_beaman_what_does_it_take_to_change_a_mind

28 The Youth Economy Report, commissioned by gohenry, 2019

29 Akwisombe, Sarah, *The Money Is Coming: Your Guide to Manifesting More Money*, Piatkus, 2020

30 Seal, Clare, *Real Life Money: An Honest Guide to Taking Control of Your Finances* and *The Real Life Money Journal*, both Headline Home, 2020

31 Holder, Alex, *Open Up: The Power of Talking About Money*, Serpent's Tail, 2019

32 https://www.vogue.com/article/parents-explain-to-kids-why-they-work

33 Moran, Caitlin, *More Than a Woman*, Ebury, 2020

34 Wincer, Penny, *Tender: The Imperfect Art of Caring*, Coronet, 2020

35 https://motherofalllists.com/2019/05/20/work-life-balance-not-me/

36 https://www.facebook.com/DrJoshuaWolrich/videos/fact-the-poorest-10-of-uk-households-would-need-to-spend-74-of-their-disposable-/780450326061765/

37 Thomas, Laura, *Just Eat It: How Intuitive Eating Can Help You Get Your Shit Together Around Food*, Bluebird, 2019

38 Greenhalgh, Professor Trisha, and O'Riordan, Dr Liz, *The Complete Guide to Breast Cancer: How to Feel Empowered and Take Control*, Vermilion, 2018

39 https://motherofalllists.com/2017/09/25/guest-list-what-i-learned-from-breast-cancer/

40 Pooley, Clare, *The Sober Diaries: How One Woman Stopped Drinking and Started Living*, Coronet, 2017

41 https://motherofalllists.com/2021/01/08/my-experience-as-the-child-of-an-alcoholic/

42 https://www.psychologytoday.com/intl/blog/fighting-fear/201402/demanding-apology?amp

43 https://www.ted.com/talks/worklife_with_adam_grant_bonus_relationships_at_work_with_esther_perel?language=en&referrer=playlist-worklife_with_adam_grant_season_3

44 https://www.nytimes.com/2020/05/08/smarter-living/how-not-to-apologize-in-quarantine.html

45 Jung, Carl, *Psychological Types*, Routledge, 1921

46 Doyle, Glennon, *Untamed: Stop Pleasing, Start Living*, Vermilion, 2020

47 https://motherofalllists.com/2020/02/10/tips-on-how-to-talk-to-your-kids-about-sex/

48 https://motherofalllists.com/2018/04/20/what-death-has-taught-me/

49 Sagan, Carl, *Cosmos: The Story of Cosmic Evolution, Science and Civilisation*, Abacus, 1983

50 https://www.ted.com/talks/chidera_eggeure_what_a_time_to_be_alone_releasing_the_fear_of_being_alone

51 Brown, Brené, *Daring Greatly: How the Courage to Be Vulnerable Transforms the Way We Live, Love, Parent and Lead*, Penguin Life, 2012

52 Soko, Ovie, *You Are Dope: Let the Power of Positive Energy into Your Life*, Quadrille, 2020

INDEX

INDEX